EARLY COBOURG

Featuring settlement, local
government and a variety of other
events and records.

Primary sources used extensively

Best Wishes
Percy L. Climo

Percy L. Climo

Early Cobourg
© Percy L. Climo
ISBN 0-9692131-0-7

Published by
Percy L. Climo

Printed and bound in Canada by
Haynes Printing Co. (Cobourg) Limited
880 Division Street, Cobourg, Ontario.

CONTENTS

INTRODUCTION   1

I/ **PRESETTLEMENT**   3

   Geology and Geography   3

   Indigenous People   3

   The Europeans   3

   Canada Day, 1791   4

   Indian Treaty   4

   Preparations for settlement   4

   Upper Canada   5

   Origin of Township Names   5

   John Graves Simcoe   6

   Township Settlement Schemes   7

   Some notes on Township grants   7

   The Township Surveys   8

II/ **SETTLERS MOVE IN**   11

   Letter of Elias Jones   11

   Lists of Settlers   12

   The 1799 Return of A. Jones   12

   July 1st, 1799 – Minutes of Council   75

III/ THE FIRST SETTLER
IN THE TOWN OF COBOURG — 17

The Group of Seven Settlers — 19

The Herriman Story — 22

Elias Jones Jr. — 30

IV/ THE NEWCASTLE DISTRICT — 33

1804 Population, District of Newcastle — 35

V/ LOCAL GOVERNMENT — 37

Duties of Parish and Town Officers — 38

The District Court House — 41

VI/ THE COMMUNITY — 43

The Start of Cobourg — 45

The First Industry — 48

VII/ A NEW ERA BEGINS — 51

The Naming of Cobourg — 51

Early Schools — 52

Property Purchases — 54

The First Sub-Division — 56

The Waterfront — 56

Some New Arrivals — 57

Cobourg Harbour — 57

VIII/ THE STAR IS BORN — 59

The Year 1831 — 59

The Cobourg Fire Department — 61

Police Villages of Cobourg and Amherst — 61

The Great Migration — 63

Cobourg's First Hospital — 64

The Steam-Boat "COBOURG" — 63

Cobourg Prospers — 65

Methodists build Cobourg's first sidewalk   65

The Presbyterians   66

Citizen Meetings   66

The Cobourg Elective Police Bill   67

The Cobourg Railway Company   67

Clergy Reserves   68

IX/ Again, INCORPORATION OF COBOURG   71

The Act of Cobourg's Incorporation   72

The First Town Election   81

The First Cobourg By-Laws   82

The New Town   88

The Public Market   88

Improvements in Cobourg   90

Queen Victoria   92

The Rebellion   92

The Cobourg Rifles   93

The First General Account of the Town of Cobourg   94

Coronation of Queen Victoria   97

Militia Activated   97

Cobourg Churches   98

A Strange Twist   99

Town Affairs   99

Shin-Plasters   101

The Marriage of Queen Victoria   101

The Stage Coach King Advertises   102

X/ THE LARGER SPHERE OF COMMUNITY   103

The New District Council   104

District Divided   105

XI/ A COLLECTION OF ITEMS – 1837-1848   107

XII/THE FLOURISHING FORTIES

XII/ THE FLOURISHING FORTIES 119

The Cobourg Board of Trade 119

The Cobourg Curling Club 120

James Gray Bethune 122

The Cobourg Harbour Company 123

West End Industry 124

The Ontario Mills Woolen Factory 126

List of Merchants – 1848 127

The Queen's Birthday – 1848 129

Some Interesting Statistics 131

Agricultural Societies 132

Local Improvements in Cobourg 133

Responsible Government 134

The New Municipal Bill 137

The First Cobourg Council 139

An Act to Vest the Harbour of Cobourg
in the Municipality of that town 139

Cobourg's 1850 Who's Who 145

Tidal Wave at Cobourg 146

A Closing Story 147

PREFACE

From boyhood, the writer has retained a certain fondness, an attachment, and good will for the Town of Cobourg. These feelings have deepened as I grew older, and for good reasons.

In my younger years, the town and its people provided an environment that was healthy, wholesome and instructive. Cobourg was a good place to develop, to grow and to mature; all preparatory for moving out into the larger community.

My father retained similar feelings. He was born in the Duchy of Cornwall, Great Britain, and he was still a babe-in-arms when our family came to and settled in Cobourg. He lived out the rest of his life in the town and often took delight in recalling stories of Cobourg happenings and his experiences of by-gone years. As told to the writer, his stories made an impression, developed a fondness for Cobourg history, and inspired the desire to ascertain more knowledge of events of earlier years.

Retirement years have opened the door to study, research, recording and writing about Cobourg's past. Today, through library and archival records, through facilities of recent years that were not available to earlier writters, one can penetrate the past and record many earlier events. This, the writer has had much pleasure in doing. The accompanying history on early Cobourg is the culmination of much study and research. Hopefully, it will assist the reader in gaining a little better insight into the story of Cobourg's developing years.

The writer was born in downtown Cobourg in the year 1906. Our family lived in the rooms above my father's store, located on King Street to the west of George Street. I still retain many fond memories of my young boyhood gained in those early and impressive years of living in Cobourg's core. Within six years of my birth, my father sold his business and the family took up residence in the extreme west end of the town. The writer lived here until manhood. He advanced through Cobourg schools, attended Church services and activities regularly, and along with neighbourhood companions had an active boyhood and youth, in enjoying to the full the various things that were healthful and helpful in the growing up process.

My teachers through the grades of the town's public school and the Collegiate Institute were excellent. The people who gave direction and leadership in the churches, imparted to their followers something that was vital and very important towards assisting one to grow and develop along lines that would be most beneficial in later life. All this is recalled in grateful memory.

Cobourg, in my impressive years, provided an environment that was healthy, wholesome, instructive and of a high quality, an excellence one usually does not find in larger centres of population.

Percy L. Climo
January, 1985.

INTRODUCTION

It was Dominion Day, July 1st, 1914. It was the forty-seventh anniversary of Canada's Confederation. It was a public holiday. Stores in Cobourg were closed for the day and citizens were active in various pursuits. The province had just emerged from a strenuous election. A local newspaper was too fully occupied, in letting off political steam, to even notice the activities of the day.

July the First, 1914, was also the seventy-seventh birthday of the Town of Cobourg. Few people, if any, realized this fact. The generation that had brought about the incorporation of the town had long since passed on. The older folk, through time, had lost track of certain earlier events. The written record, the printed word, rested in vaults, in old newspapers, long since out of sight and forgotten.

July the First, 1914, found Cobourg still basking in the charm, the atmosphere of the Victorian era. The good Queen had ascended the British Throne only a few days before the town was incorporated. Her son, King Edward the Seventh had come and gone. Her grandson, King George the Fifth now occupied the throne of the Empire. The Union Jack was on display in various locations.

It was July the First, 1837, when the incorporated municipality had cut its political umbilical cord from the Township of Hamilton, and like a new-born colt, was standing shakily at first on its own legs. Now, seventy-seven years later, the town had come through a variety of experiences. It had encountered growth, prosperous times, difficult times, recessions, and times of encouragement. It had its university for over fifty years, then lost it. The town had its own railway to the North and lost that too. Through the years its harbour had been active and productive.

July the First, 1914, was the end of an era in several ways. On the lake, the schooner days were practically over. Likewise the paddle-wheel steam-boats, that plied the lake, calling at various ports, carrying both passengers and freight. Now, the new larger ferry-boat, steaming back and forth across the lake, was paramount in harbour business. The large woolen mills, ultra modern in the 1840's, and the mainstay of local economy through the years, had closed down. Negotiations were proceeding for another industry to occupy its empty buildings. The large Crossen Car Shops that had been active for over forty years had quit. The wealthy summer visitors from south of the border were back in town, bringing with them their form of gracious living, occupying their large mansions, and engaging in their endless rounds of social activities. The stores of the town were well stocked for their summer trade. The unpaved, tree-lined streets, still traversed by many horse-drawn vehicles, were becoming accustomed to the increase in the number of motor cars or automobiles. The sandy beaches in front of the town, the beautiful Victoria Park, attracted the middle-class folk on warm, sunny days. Preparations were proceeding for the continent-famous Cobourg Horse Show in August. The Victorian Era, in Cobourg, was having its final flourish.

The Mayor and Council occupied their conspicuous seats of authority without personal financial remuneration, for their public interest and service. Since its incorporation, the place had at first been the District Town, and from the year 1850, the County Town. There was a Home for Aged, and a home for the unfortunate mentally ill. The town boasted a new general hospital. Its variety of schools held a fine record since pioneer days. Three railways now crossed its boundaries, each competing for local patronage. The population had remained around the 5,000 figure for nigh on sixty years. The Townsfolk were proud of its past military achievements.

On July the First, 1914, the people of Cobourg had no reason to believe that great changes were imminent. They went about their various occupations, professions, trades, vocations in their same accustomed manner. They little realized, that far across the seas, on the European horizon, war clouds were starting to appear, and the gathering storm would permanently change the little grey town, basking in the sun by its lakeside. Behind it all, Cobourg had a unique story of its many years. It had experienced growth, and matured through a variety of experiences. It had a narrative to be told. The town had a history. . . .

I/PRESETTLEMENT

Geology and Geography

That part of the earth's crust, known as the North American Continent, particularly the north-eastern sections, through the aeons of time, has passed through a great variety of stages; upheavals, settlements, formations of table land, sediment rocks, ancient rivers, and geological changes of various kinds. The ice ages came and receded. All have left their indelible records on the face of nature. Today, we can view the results of nature's handiwork in the formation of the Great Lakes, the Precambrian Shield, and the moraine hills of Northumberland County. Today, we find the Town of Cobourg bordering the north shore of Lake Ontario, nestling in a semi-saucer shaped plain, backed up by the Northumberland hills, all in a pleasant agricultural setting, beautiful to behold.

The Indigenous People

Following the retreat of the last ice age, and the draining of the larger Lake Iroquois, when Lake Ontario came into its own setting, dense forest grew up and covered the plains and hills. The native people, later designated 'Indian', moved in to occupy, to hunt and to fish the lands, lakes and rivers. For several thousand years they lived here their nomadic and outdoor life.

The Europeans

The European discoverers of North America, followed by explorers, fur-traders, merchants, priests, settlers and colonies; the conquests for new territory, and the expansion of the white man's domain, all took place in a progressive development. The localized area of Northumberland remained a solid forest and untouched. Time and events move on. The French occupation changed to British possession. The Quebec Act of 1774 created a Province from Labrador through the Great Lakes, and into the Ohio and Mississippi valleys, a huge territory.

The Treaty of Paris of 1783 again sets new boundaries for the Province of Quebec, eliminating the western portion beyond the Great Lakes. The year of 1784, and the aftermath of the American Revolution, brings to the Province the Refugees, loyal to British ideals, to settle along the shores of the Upper St. Lawrence, the Bay of Quinte, the Niagara Peninsula, and other areas of British North America. Except for a fur trading post at Smith's Creek, the local area is bypassed by these events.

Canada Day, 1791

The Indian term *'Kanata'*, meaning village or community, was believed first applied by the indigenous people to the French build-up along the north shore of the St. Lawrence, from the Ottawa River eastward. The term evolved and developed into the word *Canada,* which came into general use. The Canada Act of 1791, recognized the name officially for the first time. The Act was passed by the British Parliament on August 24th, 1791, and was applied to become effective on the 26th of December, 1791, the true date for the title, *"Canada Day"*. The Act divided the Province of Quebec into the Provinces of Lower Canada and Upper Canada. The local area became part of the latter province.

Indian Treaty

By the year, 1787, Lord Dorchester, the Governor of Quebec, ordered a treaty for land, north of Lake Ontario, and to the west of the Trent River. Sir John Johnson, the Superintendent General and Inspector General of Indian Affairs at that time, met with Indian representatives at the Carrying Place, at the head of the Bay of Quinte, on the 23rd of September, 1787. The lands conveyed to the Crown by treaty extended from the Carrying Place, along the North shore of Lake Ontario to the Etobicoke River, with a depth of ten to twelve miles. The land was paid for in goods, delivered at the time. The wording of this treaty was either lost, or it was left unrecorded. The boundaries were not settled until 1788. On the First of August, 1805, another deed was signed to complete the purchase made in 1787. By 1790, settlement along the Bay of Quinte had reached along the shore to the Trent River.

Preparations for Settlement

In anticipation of increased settlement, and in preparation for the dividing of government responsibilities, instructions were issued by the Government at Quebec, to Mr. Augustus Jones, Deputy Provincial Surveyor, to mark out eleven townships, bordering the north shore of Lake Ontario, from the River Trent westward to the Humber River. Jones and his party set out from Niagara in late June, 1791, and on July 1st, started from the Humber River and proceeded eastward, along the lake shore, running out a measured traverse to the western boundary of Sidney Township, located on the east bank of the River Trent.

After calculating the latitudes and departures of this traverse, Jones plotted where the respective township boundaries were to be located. On July 29, 1791, he returned westward marking out the base line and the positions of side lines for one mile inland from the lake, for each of the eleven townships. This survey ·was the first for Northumberland County and the Township of Hamilton. Hamilton Township was marked off in this manner in August, from the 13th to the 17th.

Upper Canada

The Canada Act, passed by the British Government on the 24th of August, 1791, formed the Provinces of Lower and Upper Canada from the former province of Quebec. The Act became effective as of December the 26th, 1791. John Graves Simcoe had been appointed Lieutenant Governor for Upper Canada, and arrived at Quebec on November 11th, 1791, in preparation to assume that office, where he spent the winter and spring months. He had no official power outside of Upper Canada.

It was July 8th, 1792, when he took the oath of office at Kingston. There, he appointed his Executive Council, set up the ridings or electoral districts, and appointed civil officers, both judicial and ministerial. It was his decision to hold parliament at Niagara, making Newark the capital. It was at Newark the first parliament met on September 17th, 1792, with sixteen elected representatives. Northumberland was grouped with Hastings and Lennox counties as an electorial district for that First Parliament, and the elected representative was Hazelton Spencer.

In the year 1792, Northumberland County was still a virgin forest without settlers. The policies formulated, the Acts that became law, passed by that first and subsequent legislatures, had far reaching effects in the later history of Northumberland County, Hamilton Township and indeed the Town of Cobourg. Some of these consequences will be mentioned and referred to later in this history.

Origin of Township Names
(Reference – The Cobourg World Newspaper, October 7, 1893- 6:3.)

"From an interesting historical sketch of the County of Northumberland, written by the Rev. D. Sutherland, M.A., and published in the Warkworth Journal, we quote the following which is specially of local interest:

"Murray Township was named after the celebrated General Murray, who aided Wolfe in the capture of Quebec. On the death of his heroic leader of the Plains of Abraham, he assumed command of the army, took possession of the city and strengthened its defences, and was subsequently appointed under the military regime of those days to administer the affairs of the Colony.

"Cramahe Township was named after H.T. Cramahe, who at first held a subordinate position as an official under General Murray. On the return, however, of Sir Guy Carleton (Lord Dorchester) to England, he was appointed Governor during his absence ad interim. In Garneau's History of Canada there appears an order signed by Cramahe on the Paymaster General for three month's payment for the 78th Regiment. It may be interesting to note the following daily payments as ordered by him:

	Pounds	s	d.
56 Sergents at 1s per diem	5	16	0.
56 Corporals at 8d per diem	1	17	4.
28 Drummers at 8d per diem	0	18	8.
1,195 Privates at 6d per diem	29	17	6.
Total for one day	35	9	6.

"Haldimand Township was named after General Haldimand who succeeded Carleton as Governor. Haldimand was a Swiss by birth, but he had long served in the British Army. He is described as a veteran soldier, severe in nature, imperious in manner, well fitted to lead battalions to battle, but not so well suited to exercise civil functions. The times being critical, his regime was repressive, rather than popular, and has been severely criticized by historians.

"Hamilton Township was named after Haldimand's Successor, as Governor, Henry Hamilton, Esq., who administered satisfactorily the affairs of the Colony, until he was succeeded by Colonel Hope.

"From the above historical references, it appears that the four townships of Northumberland, on the margin of the lake proceeding from East to West have been respectively named after four British rulers who held the highest office in near succession. The remaining inland townships of Percy, Alnwick and Seymour derive their names from places and families in the County of Northumberland, England."

John Graves Simcoe

Simcoe as Lieutenant Governor of a large territory, mostly of unbroken forest and three small areas of settlement — St. Lawrence and Bay of Quinte; Niagara and Detroit River area — had a formidable task to perform. He had had some earlier experience as a military man in the American Colonies and he had observed some of the settlement problems in the New England States. As a man, Simcoe was English to the core. He believed Upper Canada should be designed on a model of English Society with an aristocracy, a privileged school system, an established Church of England, and a paternalistic form of government. Simcoe was a dedicated promoter and an active planner in various schemes to advance the province. He strongly encouraged and desired a fast build-up of settlement. He promoted agriculture, opened roads, and ordered lay-outs of town sites. He was dependent upon immigration from the United States, people who were accustomed to pioneering. All these features characterized the legislation passed by the early sessions of the parliament of Upper Canada in the 1790's.

Township Settlement Schemes

In the American Colonies various schemes of settlement had evolved. For example, a tract of land, such as a township, was given over to an individual, or agent, who on organising and bringing in a certain number of settlers, allocating them to farm-size lots, received the balance of the tract, or township as his own as a reward for services rendered. Land was wealth in pioneer days. In some cases such a plan was very successful, especially when the group of settlers were of the same religious denomination or of the same ethnic class with all interested in living in their own community. Unfortunately some agents, following dishonest practices, created severe problems, hardships and misery for the victims of their schemes.

After the first parliament met in 1792, Simcoe was induced to allocate townships in Upper Canada to agents for settlement. The Lieutenant Governor had observed the practices and mal-practices of land agents in his earlier years, and he came to abhor, to detest the American settlement schemes. Nevertheless in a six month period, some thirty-six townships in Upper Canada were set aside for settlement by agent. Simcoe had hopes that the scheme would produce a build-up in population. He became disappointed on learning that some of the agents were attempting to sell their townships wholesale in the United States. The practice was discontinued, and no additional townships were offered to agents.

Most of the townships in Northumberland County came under the settlement by agent scheme. In the year of 1793, Northumberland was still an unbroken forest and not surveyed for settlement.

Joseph Keeler, of Vermont, is reported to have finally settled at what is today the Village of Lakeport in 1793. He became a settlement agent for the area. He had an agreement with Simcoe, most likely a verbal one, the terms of which we do not know.

Some Notes on Grants of Townships for Settlers

(Reference: Land Settlement in Upper Canada. 16th Report – Dept. of Archives for Ontario. By Alexander Fraser, M.A.: LL.D; etc-1920

"In May of 1796, a proclamation had been issued declaring certain grants of townships null and void, because of failure to comply with the Conditions of Settlement."

"Prior to that event, in August of 1795, the Surveyor General had reported to the Council that no settlers, as yet, had been placed on the Townships of Clarke or Cramahe by persons to whom they had been granted. The Council forthwith rescinded the grants and threw open the townships."

"In August of 1797, Surveyor-General Smith laid before the Council, a report on grants of townships, and as a result the Council submitted to the President a number of comments:

"First – They drew attention to the fact that persons obtaining such grants rarely understood in full the conditions attached to them." (Added note – Were these conditions spelled out in writing or verbal?)

"Many appeared to think that after settling forty families in a township on 200 acre lots, the rest of the land was their own."

"Others, although they understood their obligations to settle two hundred families on 200 acre lots, yet considered themselves free to sell out at anytime."

"Still others believed that after settling the two hundred families, they, in some fashion, could acquire personal holdings beyond the 1,200 acres maximum."

"The Council members were fully satisfied that there was no foundation whatsoever for any of these impressions; on the contrary they were convinced that in all such grants, the nominee was entitled only to 1,200 acres himself, with the same quantity for each of his three principal associates. Of several nominees examined by the Council, none could state any grounds on which more was expected, save general report and hearsay."

"The original principles upon which the township grants were based had never been lost sight of, nor had there ever been any idea of giving more than 200 acres to each settler." etc.

The Township Surveys

By 1795 some settlers were moving into Northumberland County. Murray Township was receiving people from the Bay of Quinte area. Further west, Cramahe and Haldimand Townships were attracting newcomers. The central government moved quickly to prepare the land for settlement, and in the summer of 1795, two survey parties were assigned to mark out the boundaries of Hamilton, Haldimand and Cramahe Townships. Mr. W. Hambly and his party worked first on Hamilton Township. They started at the south-west corner, at Gage's Creek, re-ran the original base line laid out by Augustus Jones in 1791, then proceeded to mark out the east boundary, the ninth concession and a portion of the north boundary. The line between Hope and Hamilton had been laid out earlier by a Mr. Iredel. Aaron Greeley and his cousin, Zaccheus Burnham had moved from New Hampshire to Haldimand in 1795. Greeley served on the W. Hambly survey party.

Hambly's notes made no reference to settlers in Hamilton Township. Mention is made of the (Mydndert) Harris family in Hope Township who supplied provisions for the surveyors.

In the year of 1796, Aaron Greeley supervised the marking out of lots and concessions in Haldimand and Cramahe Townships. His survey notes for this work are available. The Greeley family story mentions that he also surveyed the lots and concessions for Hamilton Township. The latter record is not available, and it is assumed to be lost or destroyed. Thus the townships were made ready to receive settlers and assign them to designated lots.

II/SETTLERS MOVE IN

The years 1796 and 1797 saw more settlers moving into Northumberland County. Some came from the Bay of Quinte, some from New Hampshire, Vermont, New York State and other United States points. The townships were still under the supervision of agents, or at least that was the general impression. Officially, Cramahe Township had been declared open in 1795. Joseph Keeler was joined by Aaron Greeley, and Asa Danforth, with the assistance from others, to bring in newcomers. It appears the agent made contact with the prospective settlers and assigned them to selected lots. To gain a patent, or full ownership of land, a newcomer had to perform certain clearance duties, build shelter, and pay a fee to the government. Apparently, no location tickets were issued to settlers brough in by agents. From the Greeley story, the agents, Greeley in particular, had made some special contract or arrangement with Simcoe, possibly a verbal agreement. Lieutenant-Governor Simcoe left Canada in September of 1796. Any verbal agreements went with him, and were not honoured by officials who carried on after his departure.

Letter of Elias Jones to the Honourable D.W Smith, 1797

Township of Hamilton
June 3d., 1797

Dear Sir:

I take the Liberty to inform you that we have thirty-seven actual settlers in the Township of Hamilton and a number more in the Township that have taken lots, but have not got on yet to work.

Expect to be at York in a few days and shall return the Letters, Names and Number of Lots they improve.

I am Sir, your most obt. Servant,
Elias Jones, Jr.
One of the proprietor agents.

The Honourable David William Smith, Acting Surveyor General,
Archives of Ontario.

Lists of Settlers

Simcoe departed from Canada in September of 1796, due to ill health. He expected to return, but circumstances arose that detained him. He never returned to Canada. For a while the central government of Upper Canada was administered by an executive committee who decided to finalize the agent-township settlement schemes and to throw open the townships so held to regular settlers. In June of 1797 "Asa Danforth and Aaron Greeley attended personally as agents to the Townships of Haldimand, Hamilton, Percy and Cramahe, and produced lists of settlers in each township." A total of 172 names were submitted for the four townships. In September of 1797, Keeler, Greeley and Danforth again visited the Committee and submitted a revised list of 201 names.

The Executive Committee refused to accept these lists of names as legitimate settlers, claiming false entries, etc. This action of the Committee placed a cloud over the lists of 1797. The government ordered Augustus Jones, Deputy Surveyor, to visit the townships of Hope, Hamilton, Haldimand, Cramahe and Percy and report on actual settlement. The 1797 lists of settlers apparently cannot be relied upon as being authentic.

Augustus Jones visited the townships as instructed. He called on each settler, recorded the amount of land cleared, and other facts, and reported to his superiors on May 1st of 1799. The writer has reviewed each parcel of land in the Registry Offices and we report the date the patent was issued and to whom the deed was given. The list for the Township of Hamilton follows:

The Augustus Jones Return May 1st, 1799

Hamilton Township

1. ABBES; Nathaniel – Lot No. 6, 1st Concession. About three acres clear. (Patent issued January 3, 1809 to John Wallis.)

2. ASH; George – Lot No. 12, in front. About fifteen acres clear. (Patent issued Sept. 15, 1803 to George Ash.)

3. ASH; George, Jr. Lot No. 13, in front. About seven acres clear. (Patent issued May 17, 1802 to George Ash Jr. All of B. Patent issued May 17, 1802 to George Ash, Sr. S. 1/2 of A.)

4. ASH; James – Lot 12, 1st Concession. About three acres clear. (Patent issued May 17, 1802 to James Ash.)

5. ASH; Joseph – Lot No. 10, in front. About six acres clear. (Patent issued March 11, 1805 to Roger Wolcott.)

6. ASH; Samuel – Lot No. 9, in front. About twelve acres clear. (Patent issued July 15, 1803 to Samuel Ash.)

7. BURGART; Moses – Lot No. 27, 3d Concession. About three acres partly clear. Living in the States. (Patent issued October 13, 1803 to Joel Culver.)

8. CHAPLAIN; Joseph – Lot No. 34, 4th Concession. About five acres clear. (Patent issued April 30, 1808 to Nancy Vaughan.)

9. CHAPLAIN; Joseph Jr. – Lot No. 22, 5th Concession. About five acres clear. (Patent issued Jan. 3, 1826 to King's College.)

10. DEANE; Noah – Lot 26, 2nd Concession. About six acres partly clear. (Patent issued Sept. 21, 1804 to Noah Dean.)

11. FERRIS; David – Lot No. 29, 3d Concession. About three acres partly clear. (Patent issued June 24, 1803 to David Ferris.)

12. GEROME; Asahel – Lot No. 7 in front. About sixteen acres clear. (Patent issued April 21, 1808 to Ashail Jerome "B", and S. Part of "A".)

13. GIFFORD; Humphrey – Lot 27, 1st Concession. About six acres clear. (Patent issued May 26, 1804 to Humphrey Gifford.)

14. GIFFORD; Samuel – Lot No. 23, 1st Concession. About three acres clear. (Patent issued Sept. 24, 1803 to Robert McDowell.)

15. GOHEEN; Thomas – Lot No. 35, 2nd Concession. About eight acres clear. (Patent issued April 19, 1808 to Thomas Goheen.)

16. GRIFFINS; William – Lot 33, 3d Concession. About one acre clear. (Patent issued May 17, 1811 to William Griffes.)

17. HAGERMAN; Abraham – Lot No. 33, 1st Concession. About seven acres clear. (Patent issued October 31, 1803 to Isaac Hagerman.)

18. HAGGERMAN; Isaac – Lot No. 29, 1st Concession. About four acres partly clear. Living in the States. (Patent issued November 4, 1803 to Isaac Hagerman.)

19. HARISON; Nathaniel – Lot No. 17, in front. About eight acres clear. (Patent issued Jan. 29, 1806 to Nathaniel Herriman.)

20. HARRIS; Bolton – Lot No. 32, 4th Concession. About one acre clear. Living in the Bay of Quinte. (Patent issued June 21, 1816 to Boltus Harris.)

21. HARRIS; Joseph – Lots No. 32 and 35, 1st Concession. About seven acres clear. (Patents issued in 1806 and 1803 to Joseph Harris.)

22. HIX; Joshua – Lot No. 31, 1st Concession. About one acre clear. Living at the Bay of Quinte. (Patent issued Sept. 19, 1805 to Jusua Hicks.)

23. HULL; Eli – Lot No. 7, 1st Concession. About five acres clear. (Patent issued Sept. 13, 1806 to Eli Hull.)

24. JONES; Elias – Lots No. 19 and 20 in front. About 12 acres clear. (Patents issued May 17, 1802 to Elias Jones.)

25. MARTIN; Moses – Lot No. 18, 1st Concession. About six acres clear. (Patent issued May 17, 1802 to Moses Martin.)

26. MARVENE; Samuel – Lot No. 20, 5th Concession. About three acres clear. (Patent issued Jan. 3, 1826 to King's College.)

27. McKEYS; Daniel – Lot No. 19, 1st Concession. About one acre clear. (Patent issued Dec. 14, 1804 to Daniel McKeyes.)

28. NICKERSON; Eluid – Lot No. 16, in front. About 10 acres clear. (Patent issued May 17, 1802 to Eluid Nickerson.)

29. NUGEN; John – Lot No. 22, 1st Concession. About two acres clear. (Patent issued September 5, 1803 to Pevoy Jones.)

30. PARKER; Samuel – Lot No. 1, 1st Concession. About two acres partly clear. Living at the Bay of Quinte. (Patent issued May 4, 1807 to Samuel Parker.)

31. PERRING; Frederick – Lot No. 18, in front, about two acres partly clear. (Patent issued June 21, 1819 to Nathan Williams.)

32. PURDY; Gilbert – Lot No. 4, in front, about three acres clear. (Patents issued to three people in 1857.)

33. PURDY; Joseph, Sr. – Lot No. 3, in broken front, about ten acres clear. (Patent issued March 20, 1801 to Thomas Fleming.)

34. ROBBINS; John – Lot No. 13, 1st Concession. About three acres clear. (Patent issued Nov. 21, 1808 to John Robbins.)

35. SMADES; Luke – Lot No. 34, 2nd Concession. About eight acres clear. (Patent issued Nov. 8, 1808 to Luke Smades.)

36. STANDCLIFFE, Stanborough P. – Lot No. 14, in front. About four acres clear. (Patent issued May 17, 1802 to Stanborough P. Stancliffe.)

37. STEPHEN; Stephen, Abner – Lot No. 6 in front. About ten acres clear. (Patent issued May 17, 1802 to Abner Stevens, Con. "A".)

38. TUBBS; Daniel – Lot No. 9, 1st Concession. About three acres partly clear. Living at the Bay of Quinte. (Patent issued May 17, 1803 to Daniel Tubbs.)

39. TUBBS; Frederick – Lot No. 10, 1st Concession. About three acres partly clear. Living at the Bay of Quinte. (Patent issued June 30, 1801 to Frederick Tubbs.)

40. TUTTLE; Stephen – Lot 17, 1st Concession. About seven acres clear. (Patent issued Dec. 2, 1802 to Stephen Tuttle.)

41. VAUGHAN; John – Lot No. 1, in front. About six acres clear. (Patent issued May 17, 1802 to Gilbert Storms. Part of "A"). (Patent issued April 30, 1805 to Liberty White. Pt. "A" & all "B").

Special note: Mr. Liberty White moved west with the Greeley family in 1806 and was later killed by Indians near Chicago.

42. VERNAT; John – Lot No. 32, 3d Concession. About one acre clear. Living at the Bay of Quinte. (Patent issued April 15, 1812 to John Vannatto.)

43. WOLCOTT; Roger – Lot No. 10, in the second broken front. About five acres clear. (Patent issued March 11, 1805 to Roger Wolcott, all "A".) (Patent issued Dec. 29, 1808 to Ranna Perino, all "B".)

(signed) A. Jones, D.P.S.

With respect to the 1797 lists, the term "settler" is applied in a very loose manner. Some of the people named were actual settlers, and working their holdings towards a final ownership. Others may have the lots, planning on moving in later. Still others, during the summer interval, had moved from one location to another. Others just may have been absentee holders. Settlement was in a state of flux, of change. The 1797 lists are the first or earliest records for the respective townships.

The following comments are from the Russell Papers – Volume II – Page 257:

"July 1st, 1799. Minutes of Council."

Present: Elmsley, Grant and Smith.

"Among other business, read Mr. (Augustus) Jones Return of Settlers, in the Townships of Hope, Hamilton, Haldimand, Cramahe, and Percy with several improvements. Hope – 28; Hamilton – 43; Haldimand – 53; Cramahe – 39; and Percy – 14, for a total of 177.

"The Board took into consideration the Reports made by Mr. Jones in the Townships of Hope, Hamilton, Haldimand, Cramahe and Percy, together with counter reports of Mr. Rogers, Mr. Greeley, etc.

"In perusing these reports and counter reports, the Board meets with anything but additional proofs of fraud, duplicity, and unprincipled selfishness of the original nominees of those townships, who undertook to settle them with new inhabitants, but appear to have brought into them persons already settled in the Province, and in many instances have only borrowed their names. Warrants were only to be issued to those who had performed their settlement duties." (Others were given time to complete their duties.)

III/THE FIRST SETTLERS IN THE TOWN OF COBOURG

Who was the first settler in Cobourg? This question has excited local history buffs for a long time, and perhaps it has been bandied about since settlement days. The traditional story names *Eluid Nickerson* who build his cabin on the west side of Division street and to the north a short distance from King Street. This bit of history was cited when I was a boy, over seventy years ago. The same story was told when my father was a boy in Cobourg in the 1860's. A number of local writers of history have emphasized this detail. Nickerson settled, worked out his obligations and came into possession of land on the east side of Division Street. His first cabin was located, just off his property on Herriman land, located probably in error due to the lack of correct markings. The cabin was handy to the small near-by stream and at that time, a few feet in the forest, one way or another, was of little concern. The main thrust was to erect shelter and to clear the trees.

Miss Idell Rogers, a descendent of the famous U.E.L. Rogers family, grew up with a liking and a flair for collecting and writing local history items. She was employed for many years by the Cobourg World newspaper, and after its demise served the Cobourg Sentinel-Star. Over the years she made many contacts with old line families and extracted from them stories, anecdotes, and folk lore of earlier years in this area. From time to time her historical writings appeared in the Cobourg World from the 1890's to the termination of that newspaper. In July of 1948 she started a column in the Cobourg Sentinel-Star entitled *"This is Cobourg"*, and after some fourteen months produced some 60,000 words of story. She did not confine her articles to Cobourg alone, but made many references to the area. She had her own particular style, a sort of friendly, folksy expression, and her work contains many facts well worth recording. She asserted there were settlers in Cobourg well before the year 1798, the date for the arrival of Nickerson. She named the Herriman family as having settled in 1797. Unfortunately some of the dates she applied to her other stories are in error.

Edwin Clarence Guillet, a Cobourg native, was born just before the turn of the century. His family had been long time residents of Cobourg. From early years he took a liking for early local history, and he had access to the old tomes of the *Cobourg Star* and the *Cobourg Sentinel-Star* newspapers and he used this privilege well, before this precious historical record was destroyed in the basement flooding of the printing plant in 1932. Guillet grew up to become the teacher, the scholar, and spent a lifetime writing Ontario and local history. His style was attractive and clear, and his method of recording history made for interesting reading. His research in this field of endeavour was extensive. In the year of 1948 he was the main contributor to the book *"Cobourg 1798-1948"*, at the same time Idell Rogers articles appeared in *"This is Cobourg"* column.

The two writers clashed by way of a newspaper controversy. Guillet attacked the writings of Rogers and charged her with relating area or Northumberland County material to Cobourg — a very localized place. Also her dates for settlement and settlers before 1798, and various other historical points came under fire. Rogers retaliated by re-asserting and naming the arrival of settlers in the early 1790's, and on other historical points. The controversy was continued off and on over several months.

It turned out to be one of those issues where both were right on some points and both were wrong on others. Nevertheless there is much value in the writings of both, and we are grateful to them for their efforts in local historical presentation.

With regards to the dates of the arrival of various first settlers, both writers failed to mention that in the settlement of this area, the townships up to 1797 were under agent supervision and no location tickets were issued by them. At least the location ticket record is not available. The agents turned in their lists of settlers giving names, lot and concession numbers, in both the June and the September lists of 1797. These lists are under a cloud due to the rejection by central government officials and are not authentic, yet may have some truth. The Augustus Jones return of May 1st, 1799 is authentic and reliable and gives the names, lot and concession numbers plus the acres cleared to that date. This list is of interest, and the names given for what later became the Town of Cobourg in 1837 are as follows:

Stephen Tuttle - Lot No. 17, Concession - seven acres cleared. Registered for patent in 1802.

Moses Martin - Lot No. 18, Concession I, six acres cleared. Registered for Patent in 1802.

Daniel McKeyes - Lot No. 19, Concession I - one acre cleared. Registered for Patent in 1804.

Stanborough P. Stancliffe - Lot No. 14, South Half of Concession "A" and Concession "B" - four acres cleared. Registered for Patent in 1802.

Eluid Nickerson - Lot No. 16, Concessions "A" and "B". Ten acres cleared. Registered for Patent in 1802.

Nathaniel Herriman – Lot No. 17, Concessions "A" and "B". Eight acres cleared. Registered for Patent in 1806.

Elias Jones, the younger – Lots Nos. 19 and 20, Concessions "A" and "B". Twelve acres cleared. Registered for Patent in 1802.

Thus we have seven verfied settlers in what later became the Town of Cobourg in 1837. These same seven names are on the 1797 Agent list for Hamilton Township. When did they actually move in? It is doubtful if one can pinpoint the year and date.

Similarly for the first settler to arrive in Hamilton Township. Varioius claims made years later by descendent families may be difficult to prove.

The Group of Seven Settlers

Stephen Tuttle's lot was north of Elgin Street and west of Division Street consisting of 200 acres. The 1804 Census list records three boys and two girls in the family. Apparently Stephen died later that year as the 1805 Census records Elizabeth as a widow. The Tuttle family surname disappears from Census listing after the year 1808. We have no further family details.

Moses Martin was located on the lot to the west of the Tuttle property and east of Ontario Street. The 1804 Census has no listing, and we have no information about this early settler. Later his lands were sold in the 1820's.

Daniel McKeyes property was also north of Elgin Street. Daniel and his wife were elderly folk with a son included in the family listing. He sold this lot of 200 acres in 1805 to Asa Burnham and moved to other land he owned in Hamilton Township. Daniel died about 1814. The McKeyes surname plays a prominent part in early Hamilton Township.

Stanborough P. Stancliffe took up land to the east of D'Arcy Street. The 1804 Census record tells us he was a family man with three boys and five girls. After the 1808 listing his name disappears from the Township Census lists and his property was sold about that time. We have only meagre details on this man and his family.

The ancestors of *Eluid Nickerson,* the local settler, lived in Norwich, England. One, a Thomas Nickerson, has dates circa 1515-1585. Another Thomas Nickerson, 1542-1599, and William Nickerson, still in Norwich, dates 1570-1625. William (Red Stocking) Nickerson, of Norwich, England, 1605-1689, married Ann Busby and emigrated to Monomoit, (Chatham) Massachusetts in the year 1637, and lived on Cap Cod, Massachusetts about 1645. This William had a family of ten children. The first child was named Nicholas, and the tenth child's name was William Nickerson. This William begat Thomas, who in turn begat Nathaniel whose wife was Annie. Nathaniel begat Eluid who was born at Danbury, Connecticut in December of 1760, who later became Cobourg's settler. Briefly, this is the Nickerson family background, courtesy Roger N. Nickerson of Toronto.

Unfortunately, at the time of this writing, this author does not have the Eluid

Part of Hamilton Township in 1799

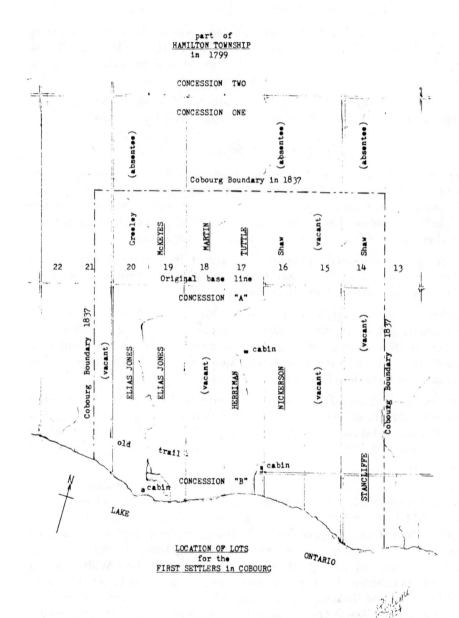

part of
HAMILTON TOWNSHIP
in 1799

CONCESSION TWO

CONCESSION ONE

(absentee)   (absentee)   (absentee)

Cobourg Boundary in 1837

Greeley McKEYES MARTIN TUTTLE Shaw (vacant) Shaw

22   21   20   19   18   17   16   15   14   13

Original base line

CONCESSION "A"

Cobourg Boundary 1837   (vacant)

ELIAS JONES   ELIAS JONES   (vacant)   HERRIMAN   NICKERSON   (vacant)   (vacant)   Cobourg Boundary 1837

cabin

old   trail

cabin

CONCESSION "B"   cabin   STANCLIFFE

cabin

N

LAKE

ONTARIO

LOCATION OF LOTS
for the
FIRST SETTLERS in COBOURG

Nickerson story, and details of the places he lived, of his education, his experiences, when and where he married, and the movements he made with his family, prior to settling in Hamilton Township.

The book, "Loyalists of Ontario," by William D. Reid lists the Eluid Nickerson family on Page 359. Nine children are recorded, all receiving grants of land as children of a Loyalist father. His wife's name was Mary, as recorded in the 1816 Hamilton Township deed of sale. The names of the children are: Nathaniel, John, Mary, Eluid, Enos, Eunice, Catherine, Levi, and David. Some of these children were probably born on the homestead. A second family, Ephriam Nickerson, appears in the 1808 and following Census lists for Hamilton Township.

Other local historians have claimed that Eluid Nickerson moved to Hamilton Township in the year of 1798. This is a very strong tradition and it is probably correct. With a large growing family and sons old enough to wield the axe, this family group in a year's time could have erected their first shelter and cleared ten acres of land, as is reported in 1799.

The Nickersons remained on their homestead until the year 1816, when they sold out the part south of King Street to Ebenezer Perry, and the north 200 acres to John Spencer. Two of the sons, Enos and Levi moved to Grantham Township in the Niagara Peninsula, to where the parents also moved. Eluid, Sr. died there in 1843 at the age of 82 years. Some of the children married and settled in other parts of Upper Canada. Other descendents took up land and lived in Hamilton Township until the 1850's.

The *Nathaniel Herriman* story is a unique account indeed. His grant of land took in 240 acres and extended from the lake north to Elgin Street, and west of Division Street. The family record reports his small house and clearing was at some distance from the lake. Behind the sandy beach fronting his lot was mostly cedar swamp with the small creek coursing down from the north. The high ground, located about three quarters of a mile from the lake, had a rich loam soil and it is most likely this was the site of the Herriman cabin and clearing. This area, during the 1920's and the 1930's was the Usher family farm and the writer recalls the richness of the soil on this farm. It is presently the site of the C.G.E. industry.

The family boat, a home-made one, apparently was stored for safe keeping in the estuary of the Factory Creek. From their cabin, they would make their way to the lake on higher ground, in a south-westerly direction, thus avoiding the cedar thickets and the low-lying creek valley on their own land.

It is quite possible the family did move in and take possession of their lot in the year 1797. Later they sold the north end of 150 acres to Mr. Moses Alley. The date of the Bargain and Sale deed is 16 July, 1808, registered on the 24th of January, 1809, with a consideration of 100 Pounds. The Herrimans sold the remaining 90 south end acres to Nathan Williams at the same time, 16 July 1808 and registered the 25th of July the same month.

A search was made in the Cobourg Registry Office for a review of these early deeds of Bargain and Sale, when Nathaniel and Bathnia Herriman sold their lot Number 17 property. The deed to Mr. Moses Alley was found and reviewed. Mr. Alley paid the 100 Pounds for the north 150 acres. The other deed to Mr. Nathan Williams was missing and not available. His 90 acres was bounded on the east by Division Street, on the north by approximately University Avenue, on the west by Spring and Hibernia Streets and on the south by Lake Ontario. This is the area in central Cobourg that is alleged to have been sold for a yoke of oxen!

It was the 29th of January, 1806, when the Herrimans received the deed of Patent for their land from the Crown.

Strange as it may seem, but the Census lists for Hamilton Township for the year 1804, the first list now available, and for subsequent years, do not record the Herriman family. The name Moses Alley does appear on these records. Apparently, Mr. Alley took over the Herriman homestead before the year 1804, and the Herriman family located elsewhere.

We give here the full account of the Herriman story, as recorded in the *Cobourg World* newspaper, hoping the reader will enjoy its contents and consider it in part history, and in part tradition and folklore.

(The Elias Jones story follows the Herriman presentation.)

The Herriman Story

The Story of Cobourg – As told in History, Folk Lore and Song.

"Lift we the twilight curtains of the past,
and turning from familiar sight and sound,"

As Whittier says, let us while perusing history's pages, cast a glance also upon tradition's shadowy tales.

"That dim strange land of old, now dying fast,
Garbed in the faded coloring of Time's tapesty."

The First Settler – Half of Cobourg sold for a yoke of oxen

In centuries to come, when Canada has become an older nation, her sons and daughters will recount with wondering, the tales of her early residents, if those who can weave strange stories now, are true to their task, and preserve them, that all may read of the heroism and adventure that marked early settlement days. Mingled with these is a folk lore that will yet compare with that of older nations.

Who is there that has heard the old song, "Tell me May How to Woo Thee," "The Butterfly, the Moth, and the Bee," a song with a moral attached: "The Moon Shines Softly O'er the Lake" "Prithee, do not frown, Sweet Lassie" or "Sally, Put the Kettle On and We'll All Take Tea", but has drawn a mind picture of the maidens of the olden days "Wearing" (as one lady who resided in Cobourg over a century ago said) "my new tibinet and all my curlings complete," seated at the harp and singing these beautiful old airs, some taken from famous operas of the time and which have a melody all their own. But if milady desired her sheet of music to have drawings, she was obliged to pay six-pence extra for it. By this was meant, that if on the fly-leaf there was a picture of Sally putting the kettle on, or of Mistress Mary in her contrary mood, to arouse the note of interpretative melody in the soloist, she must pay for this source of inspiration. These old sheets of music, the silverware with designs hammered out by hand, the quaint old books, the samplers upon which many a fair maiden sport golden hours, tell their story of the culture and refinement of many settlers who came to make their homes in the wilds of Canada. And we today honor their memory, their ability to rise above all adverse conditions, and found happy homes in a wilderness of forest trees.

A Trackless Forest

It is a little difficult to imagine the coming of the first settler to Cobourg. What was it that moved him as he came up the lake from the east probably in his little row-boat or batteau, as he evidently did for he was a U.E. Loyalist, to row into the shore, anchor his boat, and choose his future home here. We are told that the cedars grew along the water's edge in considerable density. Out on the waterfront there was probably a loon or two, and a flock of wild ducks, the deer scampered at will through the forest glades, the birds sang in the branches. This, a forest broken only by an Indian trail with one lone man setting up his hearth-stone here in the trackless wild, was the nucleus of Cobourg.

> "Our fathers to their graves have gone,
> Their strife is past, their triumph won,
> But sterner trials await the race
> Which rises in their honoured place."

But who was the first settler? Tradition and history for many years said Elias Nicholson, and perhaps it was, we can only chronicle events as they have been handed down, and leave our readers to judge.

The First Survey

The late C.C. James, a former Deputy Minister of Agriculture of Ontario, states regarding the first survey made in Hamilton Township and adjacent municipalities:

"In the year 1791, Mr. Augustus Jones, one of the assistant "Provincial surveyors, was instructed to survey the first concession line of a row of Townships from the Bay of Quinte to the present Toronto Harbour. He left Niagara on the 24th of June, 1791, and coming down the lake began work on the 5th of August in Cramahe Twp. (Correction: Jones started from the East bank of the Trent at the Sidney Township boundary), on the 9th was in Haldimand Township, and on the 13th in Hamilton Township. This latter date, therefore, gives us the first step towards providing for settlement of the Town of Cobourg and the township out of which it was formed in 1795 and 1796, the work was continued by Surveyors Hambly and Root.

This, however, does not show that there were no settlers in Hamilton Township, which for a long time included Cobourg before this date, and it is pretty certain there were a very few families. In fact this is established beyond dispute.

The Historical First Cobourg Settler

When Eluid Nicholson in 1798 erected a log dwelling where *C.P. Rall's* store now stands in the Town of Cobourg, he probably had little thought that he was helping to lay the nucleus of a town that for some years was a University (town) centre and that has long been characterized by historic memories. Little is known of him but *"The Church"* which was published at Cobourg by Dr. Bethune, in its issue of April 7, 1843, says: "Died in Grantham on the 30th ultimo, Mr. Eluid Nickerson, aged 43 years (correction: 82 years). Mr. Nickerson was one of the gallant band of U.E. Loyalists, who espoused the cause of their king at the time of the American Revolution, and who met the just reward of their hardships and privations during the eventful period in the special favour of their Sovereign, upon arrival in this province.

This is all we know of this early settler but it fixes historically the date of the coming of the first white man here. The name was first eroneously given as Elias Nicholson, but the late Mr. C.C. James, after considerable research, found the correct name in the Crown Land Records. These records also show that in Hamilton Township there was at that time other settlers.

Town Sold for Yoke of Oxen

Dr. Herriman, then residing at Lindsay, suplied an interesting article to the Cobourg Historical Society, which was in existance here some 25 years ago, from which we take the following extract:

"My grandfather received from the Government a grant of two hundred acres, now the site of Cobourg, at least in part. The North part he sold for a yoke of oxen. It was then covered with forest trees and the family occupied a small house of some kind, some distance from the lake, where they had a small clearing. In those days there were no grist mills nearer than Kingston."

The Kingston Mill was erected by the Government in 1782 or 1783, Dr. Canniff states in "His Settlement of Upper Canada," by Robert Clark who was a millwright, and for a few years the Kingston or Cataraqui mill was the only one in the province. This would place the coming of the Herriman family to Cobourg at a very early date.

It is further stated that when Aaron Greeley came from New Hampshire to Haldimand Township in 1795, that he formed an agreement with Governor Simcoe to bring in thirty settlers, furnishing them with tools, provisions, etc., and that he was to receive a large tract at Presqu'Ile and in Haldimand Township about a mile east of what is now Shelter Valley.

A grist mill was also erected very early by a settler named Keeler at what is now Colborne Harbour.

Mill at Belleville 1802

In 1802 Dr. Canniff states, Captain Myers built a flouring mill upon the Moira at Belleville, to which it is stated "Isaiah Tubbs, who lived at West Lake, came carrying a bag of grain on his back" to be ground into flour.

These dates of the building of the first mills, which should be authoritative, places the coming of the Herriman family of whom we shall give further details in another issue, at a date as early probably as that of Eluid Nickerson if not before that settler took up his abode here.

The next question that comes up is, who bought half of the Town of Cobourg and paid for it with a yoke of oxen?

Be that as it may other settlers shortly afterwards followed and it is to the color and romance of their lives here, of their sordid hard tasks and high ambitions and enterprise that we of a later generation desire to pay tribute.

– The Cobourg World, Thursday, November 27, 1924.

Note by Percy L. Climo   March 5, 1984

Mr. Frank Lapp, Editor of the Cobourg World, with whom I was personally acquainted, was an ardent history fan of old Cobourg stories. Also on the staff of The World was Idell Rogers, whose interest in local history was of a high order. The latter may have written the above story.

"Lift we the twilight curtains of the past,
  And turning from familiar sight and sound."

As Whittier sings, let us, while perusing history's pages, cast a glance also upon tradition's shadowy tales.

"That dim strange land of old, now dying fast,
  garbed in the faded coloring of time's tapestry."

For many years the name of Eluid Nickerson has been handed down as the historical first settler in Cobourg. He erected his log cabin on what is now Division Street, about where Mr. C.P. Rall's store now is. But it is known that four U.E.L. families moved from the Bay of Quinte district before 1790 to the boundary between what is now Haldimand and Hamilton Townships, three settling on the Provincial Highway in the latter township, and the other at "Kelly Hill," it seemed reasonable that there might have been settlers in Cobourg before 1798, a fact which is now firmly established. This seemed all the more probably when it is remembered that it is also historically stated that a store was opened in Cobourg in 1802.

Last November, the World printed a story contributed to the Cobourg Historical Society (now defunct) by Dr. Herriman, telling an interesting story, handed down from parent to child, of a little girl in their family being stolen by the Indians as the family were preparing to embark in a boat of home manufacture from the lakeshore here to go to Kingston to mill. Dr. Herriman stated that his grandfather received a grant of two hundred acres of land, now the site of the town of Cobourg, but that he sold the north half for a yoke of oxen. He tells the story also of the mother of the little girl who was lost, writing some verses on the sad happening, which he had seen taken from a "crack in the wall beside the old brick chimney in the living-room of a very plain and unpretentious dwelling." It was read to some interested visitor and then returned. No trace was ever discovered of the lost child.

When Dr. Herriman wrote these words he had no idea that the verses on what was probably the first tragedy in the little hamlet afterwards to be known as Cobourg, would ever be recovered. Yet this story when published in The World brought to us the information that a copy of the verses existed in a home in this county. At our request they were forwarded to us, with the comment that they were not very good verse. However, the date on which they were written, June 8, 1797, established the fact that the Herriman family were living here before Eluid Nickerson came here in 1798. There were other settlers here then also, and the "verses" tell the story of neighbours turning out to look for the child, some of whom searched through the forest, and others in their rude boats on the lake.

It is wonderful how much can be authentically ascertained in connection with the early history of the locality by getting in touch with the descendents of some of the earliest settlers.

Mother Voices Grief in Verse

When centuries ago in the depths of our forest wilds, a dusky-hued native desired to commemorate some event of foe vanquished, warrior slain or victory gained, he etched the story in symbols with a thorn on some thick-etched leaf. Others heaped up cairns of stones, raised altars, planted groves as memorials, but when the fathers of the tribes were gathered to the happy hunting ground, there were none left to tell the story of joy or grief or victory as the case might be. When this mother afar from her kindred in a new country, in a primitive home, in a trackless forest, had a great grief upon her, she recorded the story in rude verse, which was probably the first rhyme written in Cobourg. Since that time, others who have contributed to a considerable degree to the poetry of our Province, notably among whom was the late Archibald Lampman, have resided here, and sung their songs.

The rhyme may be rude which recounts the story of the lost child, but as the first probable effort at verse making made in a hamlet that was later a university town, it is worthy of being preserved.

The Lost Child – The verses are as follows:

"Verses composed by Bethany Herriman on the loss of her youngest daughter, *Diadama,* who was stolen by the Missauga Indians in the Township of Hamilton, Upper Canada, June 8, 1797. The authoress died in Forestville, Chautauqua County, New York, December 26, 1829."

"Tis in my mind to write a line
To you, my parents dear,
To let you know my grief and woe,
My Journal you shall hear.

"At my first stand on British land,
Just four weeks to a day
Before I knew the errant crew,
They stole my child away.

"Though yet unknown, which way she's gone –
We thought the woods she strayed –
The neighbours lent their friendly aid,
Great search for her was made.

"The settlers turned out volunteers,
they searched the woods all round,
But nothing of her could we hear,
She was not to be found.

"Some searched the woods by listening ear,
Thinking to hear her cry,
Some searched the lake with shining light,
I saw them sailing by."

"Some said, your child has starved to death,
Some said the lake has drowned,
Some said the wolves have taken her,
Therefore she can't be found.

"You that are parents of sweet babes,
Come sympathize with me,
Let infants stray from mother's arms,
See what their cares will be.

"My usual sleep forsook my eyes,
And I forgot to eat,
The woods were witness to my cries,
This prayer I did repeat.

"I did beseech Almighty God,
In that distressing hour,
That he would furnish me with grace
While he displayed his power.

"Come old and young of every tongue,
Come lend a secret prayer,
Ascend your cries above the skies
To ease my soul of care.

"So many years in floods of tears,
For my poor child I spent,
'Tis all in vain that I complain,
And yet I do lament.

"So now behold with troubled soul,
Before my God I fall,
He is my Faith and Comforter,
He is my all in all."

— *The Cobourg World, Thursday, April 23, 1925*

The Story of Old Cobourg

The Little Hamlet's First Tragedy (From the Cobourg World, Thursday, December 11, 1924)

In our issue of November 27, we referred to the early settlement of the Harriman family here. Mr. Harriman having been given a government grant of two hundred acres of land, where the town of Cobourg now stands, the north hundred of which he sold for a yoke of oxen. A sad tragedy happened in this family soon after their arrival which is best told in Doctor Harriman's own words. His letter to the Cobourg Historical Society said:

"My father, when a youth, emigrated from the State of Vermont, and with his parents, and three brothers, and I think three sisters, settled upon the land now occupied by the Town of Cobourg. What I shall hereafter state must be accepted as my memory preserves the traditions of the past. I recollect reading some copy of original poetry written by my father's mother, referring in what then seemed to me very good poetry of a pathetic strain to her 'Lost Child.' I regret that it was not preserved. The last recollection I have of it is, when it was removed from the usual resting in a crack beside the old brick chimney in the living room of a very plain and unpretentious dwelling. It was read to some interested friends and then replaced. It seems to me it was written in verse of four lines with a rolling low sounding rhythm, in metre or what not. It covered about a page of foolscap paper that was somewhat smoky and dingy. From these remembrances and frequent repetitions of the story of my father and others during much of my adult life, I am quite satisfied the incident of the stolen child is authentic.

Started for Mill at Kingston

"When my grandfather received a grant of two hundred acres of land, now the site of the Town of Cobourg, it was covered with forest trees, and the family occupied a small house of some kind at some distance from the lake, where they made a small clearing. In those days there was no grist mill nearer than King-ston, and settlers who were so far advanced as to have grain to be ground, were obliged to take it to that far-off place. They did not go by land but always took a boat, sometimes of rude construction - no line boats with palace saloons to travel by then.

Wood Gay with Flowers

"On a pleasant morning the family set out for a trip to Kingston. It appears to me all were to go; at least they all left the home together to go to the boat. It was natural that children would loiter along, or wander a little way off in the bush, as that time the woods were gay with spring flowers. When the family arrived at the beach one child, a little girl, was missed. The anxiety of the par-ents may well be imagined, better than described. At all events there was a rally and immediate search was made. Not seeing her readily they supposed she had wandered away picking flowers here and there and perhaps had got lost in the thicket. It must be remembered there was quite a thick cedar swamp near by. Any person who had ever attempted to make a short cut out of or through one of these tangled and densely wooded jungles will have no difficulty in realizing how easy it is to go astray and come out at the wrong place, as I have often experienced to my great discomfort.

Found Tracks in the Sand

But even this fond hope was soon dispelled when some of the searchers came upon a plot of cleared sandy soil, and observed immediately the prints of little bare feet, painfully plain, in the sand, as if on a running gait, and immediately associated with them, the impression of moccasined feet of a grown-up Indian. No other sight ever greeted their anguished eyes, or sound was ever heard to tell what had become of the lost child. There was nothing to solve the mystery but those footprints in the sand. It flashed upon the mother's mind without long reasoning that an Indian had surprised the little girl as she became separated from the rest of the company, and muffled in his blanket, was fleeted through the dense forest and out of sight and hearing, with that cunning and agility known only to the first inhabitants of our forests. I forget the child's name, but it was some quaint, old fashioned name, not however obsolete, like Martha, or Margaret, or Matilda, or Samantha.

Gathering of the Clan

"There was a Samantha Waite, the Waite's of Haldimand Township and of Whitby, where descendents of the Harriman family on the female side. So also the Pettits of Haldimand or Cramahe. Perhaps these people have now joined the multitude in the great beyond, and perhaps also the mother there found her lost child. There is a great gathering of the clan beyond the border line. I have in my home just now a fair domestic maid from among the Ojibways and Ottawas, on the Manitoulin Island, and when I received your letter of reminder, I said to my wife, "we had better use that girl well, for it is hard to tell how near a relative she is of mine."

"Although irrelevant I may state in this connection that during my several visits to the great Manitoulin and observation of some of the settlements of Indians there, amongst other things I found they were very fond of taking and adopting into their homes any white child they could legitimately secure. There were several to whom I heard they had given foster homes, and today there may be found among them many a fair rosy-cheeked child. Of course they know themselves only as Indians.

Make Good Citizens

"I had a brother of my domestic for a time as a chore boy – a better one I never had. I had him placed where he learned carriage-making. He is now a good workman and well-liked by everybody, who knows him, erect, proud, always neatly and well dressed, of good deportment and unsullied reputation. Much more might be said on the subject of these people making good citizens."

— *The Cobourg World, Thursday, December 11, 1924*

Elias Jones Jr.

Elias Jones Jr., early in 1797, petitioned the central government for the possession of Hamilton Township lots Numbers 19 and 20, in the broken front Concessions "A" and "B". The meeting of the Executive Council at York on the 17th of June, 1797, recommended the requested lots be granted to him, if vacant. This action was confirmed by the Hon. Peter Russell on the 19th of June, two days later. Thus Elias Jones came into possession and in May, 1802, received the Patent deeds for nearly 450 acres of land, which in later years became part of the Town of Cobourg. A large creek coursed its way southerly between these two lots emptying into a large estuary, a good land-locked harbour for small boats. It was early that same month when Elias Jones wrote a letter to the government, advising them of the number of settlers in Hamilton Township, and signing himself as "one of the proprietor agents." Apparently he had been active in assisting settlers to locate and used his boat for this purpose. By the time Augustus Jones made his visit in 1799, Elias Jones had some twelve acres of land cleared, probably in Lot Number 20, on the higher ground to the west of the creek valley.

Elias Jones was born in the year 1770. His place of birth, activities, and movements prior to his taking up land in Hamilton Township has not been ascertained. He was married to Margaret, daughter and fifth child of Myndert Harris. of Hope Township, possibly about the year of 1798. To this union six daughters and two sons were born.

After acquiring his land in what later became the Town of Cobourg, the writer assumes he erected his cabin on the west bank of the creek at the lakefront. In selling out his Lot Number 20 in late 1803, he retained 2-1/2 acres at the southeast angle in Concession "B", which was held after his demise in 1836 by his sons until 1845. This parcel of land was serviced for access by Monk Street, where it changed direction east of Tremaine Street, and knuckled southerly to the lake bank. From the beginning, Jones may have had overland access to his cabin by a laneway from King Street, the old trail, in the area of Tremaine Street. Over the years, much of this part of the lake bank has been eroded.

Elias Jones retained his lot number 19, located on the west side of Ontario Street until the year 1819. In the meantime he owned, bought and sold various properties in Hamilton Township. His movements are a bit obscure, but in later years he conducted a very successful, prize-winning farm about mid-way between Cobourg and Port Hope.

Elias Jones was a very active person. He was one of the first Justices of the Peace in the Newcastle District. He was an early school trustee, a member of the District Land Board, an Inspector of Distilleries and Breweries, and one of the active leaders in the early Northumberland Agricultural Society.

Elias Jones passed away June 9th, 1836. His wife and four daughters predeceased him two to four years earlier. He was in the 67th year of his age, and a highly respected citizen. Many people attended his funeral. His obituary reports:

> "A good subject, a good neighbour, a good father,
> a Christian and an honest man. He was one of the
> earliest settlers."

We have given a brief review of the seven settlers, the first to actively take up land in what later became the Town of Cobourg of 1837. Why was *Eluid Nickerson* selected, chosen and decided upon as being Cobourg's first settler by earlier local historians? A strong tradition backs up this selection. *Why?* Later in this story we will return to the subject.

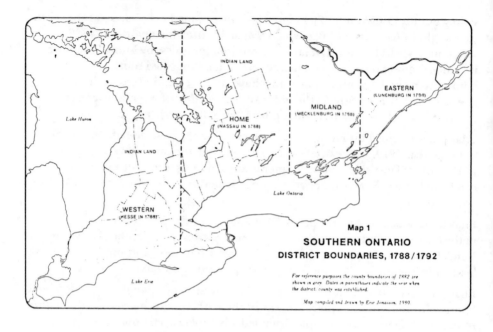

Map 1
SOUTHERN ONTARIO
DISTRICT BOUNDARIES, 1788/1792

Maps – Courtesy of *"Families"*
– The Ontario Genealogical Society

Map 2
SOUTHERN ONTARIO
DISTRICT BOUNDARIES, 1798

IV/THE NEWCASTLE DISTRICT

The earlier divisions of the Province of Upper Canada into four districts was a start, and as settlement progressed these larger areas would be sub-divided and new districts carved out in order to improve local area administration, Courts of law, land registration, etc.

An Act was passed by Parliament in 1798 "For the Better Division of the Province". The Newcastle District, embracing the Counties of Northumberland and Durham was conceived at this time and the Act included a provision for its formation as follows:

Home District XXIV - And be it further enacted by the authority aforesaid, That the counties of Northumberland and Durham, York and Simcoe, do constitute and form the Home District.

District of Newcastle to be eventually declared by Proclamation.

XXV - Provided always, and it is hereby further enacted, That when and as soon as the said Counties of Northumberland and Durham shall make it satisfactorily appear to the Governor, Lieutenant Governor, or person administering the government of this Province, that there are one thousand souls within the said counties, and six of the townships therein do hold town-meetings according to the law, then the said counties, with all the land in their rear, confined between their extreme boundaries, projected north, sixteen degrees west, until they intersect the northern limits of the Province, shall and are hereby declared to be a separate district, to be called the District of Newcastle; and the Governor, Lieutenant Governor, or person administering the government of the Province, is hereby authorized upon such proof as aforesaid, to declare the same by Proclamation, any time within one year after the same shall be so established, as to him shall seem most fit.

The reduced size of the Home District, as outlined above in XXIV, came into effect on January 1st, 1800.

The Justices of the Peace met in Quarter Sessions at York. Mr. William Jarvis was chosen Chairman. From the list of J.P's. attending the meetings, the names were from the western part of the Home District and no representation present from Northumberland and Durham.

At a meeting of the J.P's. held at York, 1st of July, 1800, David McGregor Rogers, of Cramahe Township was appointed Registrar for Northumberland County to be responsible for the registering of deeds, conveyances, wills, etc.

The next move for this area was the appointment of Constables for unorganized townships. On the 17th of January, 1801, Joseph Ash and John Vaughan were appointed Constables for Hamilton Township. The following year, 1802, John Vaughan and Nathaniel Abby were the Constables for Hamilton Township.

In unorganized townships, it was the duty of township constables to call the freeholders and householders together for the Annual Town Meeting. The meetings after the initial one were to be called by the Township Clerk. It is not clear as to when Hamilton Township held its first Town Meeting, whether in the year 1801 or 1802. These meetings appointed township officers and passed on local rules.

By early 1802, settlement in Northumberland and Durham had increased to over 1,000 people and six townships had held town meetings according to the requirements for the formation of the District of Newcastle. It was on the 23d of June, 1802, when His Excellency, Peter Hunter, Esquire, Lieutenant Governor of the Province Upper Canada issued a Proclamation that formed the Counties of Northumberland and Durham into the Newcastle District.

Next, an Act to provide for the Administration of Justice in the Newcastle District was passed on the 7th of July, 1802.

Justices of the Peace, meeting in their court of Quarter Session was first held on the 12th of October 1802, in Murray Township. Alexander Chisholm and Isaiah Hall presided at this first meeting.

THUS, with the above events, the Newcastle District was carved from the former Home District, organized and activated.

Population, District of Newcastle

The following table is compiled from the annual return of the inhabitants of the District of Newcastle, for the year 1804.

TOWNSHIPS	MALES			FEMALES			TOTALS.	TOTALS.
	ABOVE 60.	UNDER 60 OVER 16	UNDER 16.	ABOVE 60	UNDER 60 OVER 16	UNDER 16		
MURRAY	4.	35.	33.	1.	30.	25.	128.	
CRAMAHE	5.	76.	110.	-	60.	95.	346.	
HALDIMAND	5.	90.	82.	2	76.	101	356.	
HAMILTON	6.	84.	110.	3.	68.	113.	384.	
PERCY	-	34.	51.	-	29.	34.	148.	
HOPE	-	68.	84.	-	51.	72.	275.	
CLARKE	-	16.	6.	-	5.	10.	37.	
DARLINGTON	-	28.	31.	-	17.	22.	98.	
TOTALS	20.	431.	507.	6	336	472.	1,772.	

— Taken from the Town Clerks' Return, 1804
D. McG. Rogers, Clerk of the Peace

For the year 1806, the Annual Return gives a total population of 2,011.

For the year 1808, the total population for the District had risen to 2,306 inhabitants.

FIREMAN'S CERTIFICATE.

This will certify, that the Magistrates, in Quarter Sessions, satisfied of the efficiency of

R. D. Chatterton   as **Fireman** in one of the Volunteer Fire Companies established by the Board of Police for the Town of Cobourg, have accepted his enrolment as such **Fireman,** which, according to Act 7. Geo. IV. Chap. 8th exempts him and he is hereby exempted, during the period of his enrolment and continuance of actual duty as such **Fireman,** from Militia duty in time of peace, from serving as a Juryman, or Constable, and from all other Parish and Town offices.

[signature]
Clerk of the Peace.

CLERK OF THE PEACE OFFICE.

Nov 15th 1837

Copy of the Roll of the Cobourg Engine Fire Company No 1
for the Years 1839 & 1840

Peter McCallum Captain	William J Strong
Alex Strough 1st Lieut	William Barrett
Joseph Benham 2nd Do	Matthew Purser
Andrew Moorish 1st Branchman	John Brodly
Chas Perry 2nd Do	John Lumble
James McConnell 3 Do	Peter McGuire
James Hay Secty & Treasurer	John Bradburn
Robert Murray	Ephraim Powell
Nicholas Rigg	William Williams
Joseph Philip	Isaac Dobson
William Gregg	Thomas Pratt
James McDonald	James McFadden
Jacob Thompson	Joshua Howard
Charles Bellwood	George Kirkman
Thomas Sharp	
John Barr	
George Ellis Minn	
Erven Wentworth Powell	

a true list
James Hay Secretary

V/LOCAL GOVERNMENT

The District Justices of the Peace or Magistrates were appointed by the Governor in Council, the central government, and held office at the pleasure of the Governor. Their power of action was confined to inside the boundaries of their own district. They met in the Court of Quarter Sessions, that is four times each year. They held court on minor cases and had powers over and above the Town Meetings in local government.

The *Town Meeting* was a democratic process employed in the New England States. Each Township or organized community held meetings at which every citizen may vote on all questions which arise concerning the township. However, when the number of inhabitants become greater than can be contained in a meeting hall, the system breaks down.

The Loyalist settlers brought the town meeting system to Canada. In 1792, the members of the Upper Canada House of Assembly, elected by freeholders, were mostly from the American Colonies, and accustomed to local American municipal institutions, and to "local home rule" by persons elected at a town meeting, or meetings of similar character.

In 1792, at the First Parliament, these elected representatives were desirous of having such institutions established in Upper Canada by law. Some had been already operating by custom. A Bill was proposed in the legislature to this effect. Lieutenant Governor Simcoe considered such proceedings subversive to English principles. The proposed Bill was not advanced. Town meetings, as such, were not encouraged in Upper Canada. The result was, a "watered down" system of Town Meetings emerged and the lawful proceedure allowed annual town meetings in each organized township, at which officers such as Clerk, Treasurer, Assessor, Path Masters, Pound Keepters, Fence Viewers and later on, Wardens were appointed for one year. Also certain regulations were passed such as the height of fences, fees, registration of cattle marks, etc.

The Township Officers were responsible to the appointed J.P.'s. or Magistrates, meeting in Quarter Sessions in their District. The Magistrates also passed regulations for the Township Officers to follow.

Thus, from the above outline of Local Government, final authority rested with the central government with power flowing from the top down, rather than from the "grass-roots" upward.

Hamilton Township held Town Meetings from the beginning in 1801 or 1802 into 1849, when a new system of Municipal Government came into force in 1850, and the Township Councils were elected.

We now give details of the duties of Parish and Town Officers, which varied somewhat from time to time over the years the Town Meeting system was in force.

Duty of Parish and Town Officers

"The path of duty, is the path to heaven" – Pope

As the inhabitants of the new townships in this district are entirely composed of emigrants from Great Britain and Ireland, who had no parochial or public duties to perform in their native countries, they feel bewildered and at a loss when called upon to perform such duties here. From the ignorance of the nature of such offices, arises, as may be expected, mistakes, wrangles and animosities. To obviate the difficulty of obtaining correct information, and to prevent petty broils and disturbances, an abstract of the numerous Acts, which relate to parish and town officers, and which at present are scattered throughout the whole of the Statutes, might be drawn up, sent to the Town Clerks, and directed to be read in every new Township for a certain number of years, at the annual town meetings. It is at all times unpleasant for magistrates to fine, and perhaps unjust when a mistake or neglect happens through ignorance.

As a local and temporary remedy for this evil, we send you a very brief abstract of the laws on this subject for insertion in your useful paper; hoping that it will be read in the new townships with attention; and that the information which it contains will spread, and prevent strife.

In this peaceful and happy Province, the lightness of taxes, the rapid increase in the value of land, the plenty which everywhere prevails, and the security afforded to our persons and properties by the mild and equatable laws of our native country, are advantages for which we cannot be too grateful, and which ought to make us diligent and faithful in the discharge of every social and public duty. We would remind those whom these arguments fail to convince, that the money extracted from them in the shape of fines, might, at least for themselves, be more profitably employed in the purchase of sugar and tea for their wives and daughters.

The Town Clerk – keeps a book of records, in which are annually inserted the names of the town officers appointed at, the regulations made, by the town meeting. It should also contain the form of the Assessment roll, and of the collector's bond, the fees directed to be taken by pound-keepers, etc. This officer, reckoning from the time of the town meeting, is required to take the oath of office in seven days; to give notice, either personally or by writing of their appointment to the two assessors, and direct them to take the oath immediately, in ten days; to make an affidavit of his having given this notice, and send it, accompanied with the names and descriptions of the assessors and collector, to the Clerk of the Peace in twenty days; to have the collector's bond executed within a month and sent to the treasurer within two months. For these duties his fees are four dollars. The sureties or bondsmen of the collector should be substantial and responsible land holders.

The Assessors - are required to take the oath of office within ten days after their appointment; to take an assessment of all rateable property in the township, between the first Monday in February and the latter end of March; to sign their names to this assessment, put a copy up in the most public part of the township and deliver it to the Clerk of the Peace, before whom one of them must make oath to its accuracy, on or before the first day of April. The form of this roll, with a description of all rateable property, can be obtained either from the assessor of former years, the Town Clerk, or (which is the safest way) from a magistrate.

In taking every person's rateable property, they must apply to the person himself, and allow him to give it in. By refusing to give in, or by giving in too little, he is liable, upon information, a penalty of five pounds. A copy of the assessment roll being exposed to public view, every man can judge whether his neighbour has given in justly; and when a dispute arises about the quantity of land it must be surveyed.

The Assessors are also requried to take, at the same time, a list or census of all male and female inhabitants, above and under sixteen years of age, including servants. Heads of families who neglect or refuse to give in the number of their respective families for ten days after application, are subject to a penalty of eight dollars. The fees of assessors are seven per cent upon the amount of rates. No person should be appointed to this office who cannot write distinctly.

The Collector - is required to take the oath of office within seven days; to enter into bond to the treasurer of the district, with two sufficient sureties within a month; to pay over the moneys which he may collect to the treasurer, every three months, or oftener, if required, but to pay over the whole on or before the first day of January ensuing his appointment; and to levy the taxes by obtaining warrant from a magistrate, if they are refused or neglected to be paid for fourteen days after demand. The collector is allowed five percent upon the amount of his collection. This office also requires a man of some education.

The Overseer of the Highways - are required to take the oath of office in seven days; to make a list of all the inhabitants within their respective divisions, liable to perform statute labour, distinguishing those who have teams, and deliver it to the magistrates within twenty days; to call out their divisions within ten days, after being directed to do so by the Magistrates; to give three days notice (Sundays not included), either verbally or in writing, of the time, place, teams and tools which will be wanted; to account for labour, fines, etc., to the magistrates, under penalty of three months imprisonment; to take care that the roads are at all times safe and passable, or to warn people of danger; to lay out the statute labour impartially and for the good of the public; and to act as fence viewers.

Persons who wish to compound for their statute labour, must do so within three months after the appointment of the overseer. The composition is 5s. for team and driver, and 2s 6d. for a man for each day. Every man is required to bring such teams and tools as are wanted, and to work eight hours each day diligently and faithfully. The penalty for neglect is ten shillings per day for a team and driver, and five shillings for a man, with costs of prosecution. Every man from 21 to 50 years of age, not assessed, is liable to perform 3 days labour. All persons who place fences upon or encumber roads, injure bridges, etc., are liable to a penalty of eight dollars with costs; and those who neglect to remove trees, which fall upon roads out of their clearings, within twenty-four hours, may be fined 10 shillings for each day such tree obstructs the road.

When we reflect – as every man who is capable of reflection must certainly do – upon the beauty and usefulness of good roads, and when we consider that the annual labour, required by the laws of our country, conduces to our own immediate comfort, convenience, and to increase in value of our properties, we ought to require neither persuasion nor compulsion to induce us to perform this labour cheerfully, diligently and faithfully.

The Town Wardens are required to take the oath of office within seven days; to appear in behalf of the township in all civil processes which concern its interest; to bind out orphan children with consent of two magistrates; to enforce the proper observance of the Sabbath, etc.

The Duty of Pound Keepers is to take the oath of office in seven days; to impound all cattle, horses, sheep and hogs which are taken during damage, or running at large, contrary to the laws of the Province or the regulations of the Township; to put up within 48 hours, in three public places, when the damages and fees are not paid, notices describing the marks of the cattle impounded, and stating the time when they will be sold, which is 15 days after notice; to pay his own charges and the damages first, and then render the overplus to the owner.

When the parties cannot agree upon the damages, a magistrate is required to issue his warrent to three respectable men of the neighbourhood, who appraise them upon oath. Two overseers are required to decide upon the sufficiencies of the fences. A statement of the poundkeeper's fees should be furnished to them annually by the Town Clerk. No stone horses above one year old are allowed to run at large under a penalty of 20 shillings, – and no rams, from the 1st September to 20th December, under the same penalty.

Thirty overseers of roads and six pound keepers may be appointed for each township.

No person can be called upon to hold the same office in less than three years; but he can be appointed to a different one each succeeding year.

In general, the penalties, to which parish and town officers are liable for neglect of duty, range from two to five pounds for the first offence, and ten pounds for the second; not including the costs of conviction, which are considerable. When we add to these penalties a sense of duty, and the sacred obligations of an oath – two considerations which ought even to outweigh the loss of property, we hope that there are few men who, when once informed of these duties, will be so callous and insensible to all feelings of honour, interest, and religion, as to neglect them.

To conclude, there can be no object more agreeable in the sight of man, or more acceptable to the Supreme Author of all order, than a peaceful and well regulated community, of which every member is willing cheerfully and faithfully to contribute his share of duties.

"Atticus"

– The Cobourg Star, January 25, 1832

The account of the Treasurer of the Newcastle District, for the year 1831 is given on Page 31 of the Cobourg Star, February 8, 1832, and is listed above the name of E.E. Burnham, Treasurer, N.D.

The District Court House

Before leaving Canada in 1796, Lieutenant Governor Simcoe, the visionary, the planner, foresaw the time and need when the District of Newcastle would be formed and it was probably his decision to have the location of a District Town at the end of the Presqu'ile Peninsula. Consequently in 1797, orders were issued for the layout of such a townsite to be called the Town of Newcastle. The layout made provision for a district court house and various amenities needed in a district town. Lots were sold to private individuals, and after the formation of the District in 1802, a court house building was erected on this townsite.

The first court to be held in the Town of Newcastle had to be cancelled due to the disasterous loss of the government sail-boat *"Speedy"*. The Magistrates of the District never held a Quarter Session meeting there, preferring other locations. Finally, it was decided to build a courthouse in a more central location. Influenced by Asa Burnham, a J.P., a new site was finally selected in Hamilton Township in Lot Number 20, First Concession. A frame building was erected on the crest of a hill, on the east side of Burnham Street and to the north of Elgin Street. It was opened for use in 1807, and served the District until the early 1830's. Shortly after its opening, a store was located nearby, followed by hotels and houses. The local area became known as the Village of Amherst.

In 1832, a new Court House and Gaol was erected across the road on the west side of Burnham Street, on the site of the present day Golden Plough Lodge.

With the incorporation of the Town of Cobourg, on the 1st of July, 1837, the Village of Amherst became part of the new town and Cobourg also became the District Town.

The Location of the District Courthouse in Hamilton Township

The wooden structure was first used in the year 1807.

Registration of Deed to Courthouse Property

Registration instrument No. 307, dated April 16, 1812, and registered on the 4th of May, 1812, conveys two acres of land for use of Gaol and Courthouse from Asa Burnham to Alexander Fletcher et al. This parcel of land is located on the crest of the hill, on the east side of Burnham Street, and some 500 feet plus, north of Elgin Street. See accompanying sketch. It appears that the 1805 Building Committee, appointed by the Magistrates, decided on a change of location from Lot No. 19, to Lot No. 20, both owned by Asa Burnham.

The list of the District Magistrates, mentioned in the 1812 deed, is as follows:

> *Alexander Fletcher,* of the Township of Darlington
> Richard Lovekin, of the Township of Clarke
> Leonard Soper, of the Township of Hope
> Benjamin Marsh, of the Township of Hope
> Elias Smith, of the Township of Hope
> Elias Jones, of the Township of Hamilton
> Richard Hare, of the Township of Haldimand
> Joel Merriman, of the Township of Cramahe
> Benjamin Richardson, of the Township of Cramahe
> Asa Weller, of the Township of Murray

The Courthouse Property

VI/THE COMMUNITY

The early settlers, living along the lake front of Cramahe, Haldimand, Hamilton and at Smith's Creek in Hope Township formed more or less a community of interests. An early story reports that when the residents of Smith's Creek needed help to build a mill, Joseph Keeler of Cramahe and Haldimand took a group of men with him to assist in the raising of the mill. Neighbours! Susan Greeley, in her story tells us that travel went by boat in season, otherwise along the lake shore. An earlier account reports that before Northumberland and other north shore counties were settled, people travelling between the Bay of Quinte area and Niagara by land, required an Indian guide to take them through. There was an old trail along the north shore of Lake Ontario of some sort.

Of what later became Cobourg, that trail moved inland from the lake bank near the small creek, in order to avoid a cedar swamp and to ford the stream above its estuary. Similarly westward, at the larger creek, the trail crossed the stream above the high water mark of Lake Ontario. The trail continued westerly to gain the lake shore a mile or so beyond. Thus the old blazed route, trail, tote-road, or bridle path became later, what is to-day King Street West, with its frequent change in direction. In flat country no surveyor would lay out a new road like what King Street is with its changes in direction.

Eliud Nickerson selected a spot for his first cabin close by this old trail and convenient to the small creek for water supply and boat storage. Mrs. Margaret Wells, née Ash, who was born in Hamilton Township in 1803 tells us:

"The first place of business in Cobourg was a blacksmith shop which stood about where Messers Graham and Minaker's store now stands (in 1874)." This location was on the north side of King Street, to the west of the small creek, and alongside the old trail. Property deeds confirm this location, and the blacksmith's name was Jacob Firmin. His land purchase of one acre was registered in 1812, but most likely he arranged to locate long before that date. Mrs. Wells mentioned the first tavern, built by Elijah Buck, was at the south-west corner of King and Division Streets. Buck registered his land purchase in 1812, but from

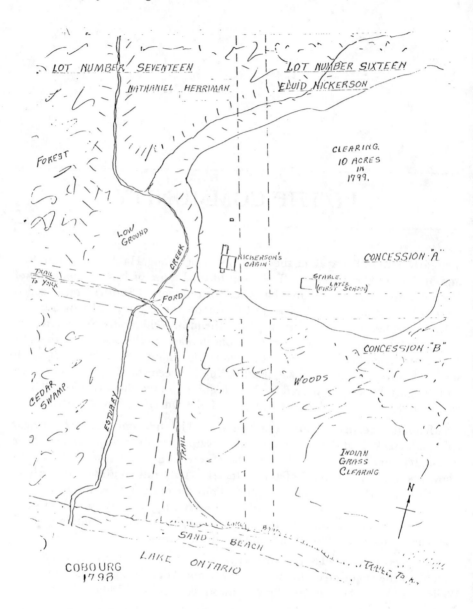

LOT NUMBER SEVENTEEN   LOT NUMBER SIXTEEN
NATHANIEL HERRIMAN   ELUID NICKERSON

FOREST

CLEARING.
10 ACRES
IN
1799.

LOW
GROUND

CREEK

CONCESSION "A"

TRAIL
TO YORK

FORD

NICKERSON'S
CABIN

STABLE.
LATER
(FIRST SCHOOL)

CEDAR
SWAMP

ESTUARY

TRAIL

CONCESSION "B"

WOODS

INDIAN
GRASS
CLEARING

N

SAND   BEACH

COBOURG
1798

LAKE   ONTARIO

TRAIL TO K.

other sources we learn that Buck arrived about the year 1810. Dr. Timothy Kittridge was around about the same time and he too was active in early land transactions, along the old trail. Mrs. Wells continues:

"The first goods sold in Cobourg were bought by Major (Elias) Jones, afterwards a man named McDonald bought goods and sold them to settlers, and then a man named Mungo or Mango opened a little store."

Jones probably used his boat to bring in a load of goods and re-sold them from his lake shore cabin. Early property deeds, dated 1816, indicated that *John Monjeau* (not Mungo) owned a lot on the south side of King Street, near the small stream. This could have been the location of the first store. Development started close by the old trail at the corner of Division Street and King Street, moving westward and later spreading out.

It now appears that the motive why *Eluid Nickerson* has been given the credit of being Cobourg's first settler, is not for the reason he was the first person to live within the boundaries of 1837 Cobourg, but because his cabin, erected in 1798, was on the site of the first build-up that later became the town. Other settler's cabins and clearings were about three-quarters of a mile distant from the start of development.

The Start of Cobourg

Mrs. White of White's Mills writes: "I was married to Mr. (Josiah) White in 1812, and came to Cobourg in 1813. It was quite a wilderness, but a few small clearings, and only three houses in the place, a rough corduroy road led to the lake."

Mrs. Wells further tells us: ". . . the first school was held in an old stable, which had been fitted up for the purpose by nailing slabs over the cracks to keep out the rain. It was taught by the daughter of a U.E. Loyalist, and stood where Waldie's bakery now stands (1874)." Mrs. Wells continued to relate that she attended this school, of how the children used to amuse themselves at noon by running down through the woods. . .or sometimes going down to the sandy beach to watch the Indians catching sturgeon. She continues: "It is curious to think of this little band of children who trudged through the woods to school, bare footed and scantily clad in such coarse raiment as the country afforded, and yet many of whom lived to see themselves surrounded by every luxury." These comments are most interesting!

The years of this first school would be about 1810 or 1812. The location of this old stable building was on the north side of King Street and a bit east of Division Street, some 100 feet or more, distant from Nickerson's first cabin, and it most likely was Mr. Nickerson's first stable, lately abandoned. Nickerson with a large growing family had probably built a new dwelling elsewhere on his property. The school teacher may have been Nickerson's daughter, Mary.

The settlers in the Cobourg area were not lacking for religious meetings and the Circuit Riders visited regularly. The early Methodists who came to Upper

Early Property Transactions
and
Lot Severances
in
Down-Town Cobourg

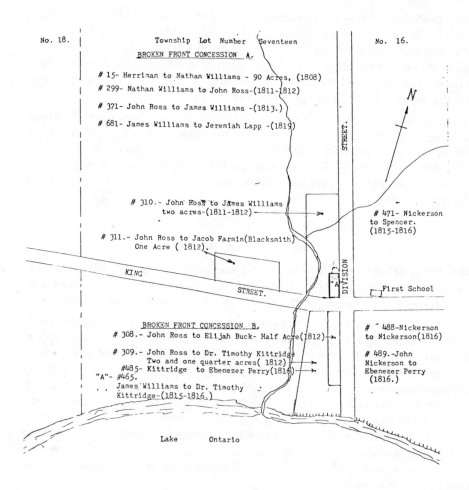

No. 18.

Township Lot Number Seventeen

BROKEN FRONT CONCESSION A.

No. 16.

15- Herriman to Nathan Williams - 90 Acres, (1808)

299- Nathan Williams to John Ross-(1811-1812)

371- John Ross to James Williams -(1813.)

681- James Williams to Jeremiah Lapp -(1819)

310.- John Ross to James Williams
two acres-(1811-1812)

471- Nickerson
to Spencer.
(1815-1816)

311.- John Ross to Jacob Farmin(Blacksmith)
One Acre (1812).

KING

STREET.

STREET.

DIVISION

"A"

First School

BROKEN FRONT CONCESSION B.

308.- John Ross to Elijah Buck- Half Acre(1812)

309.- John Ross to Dr. Timothy Kittridge
Two and one quarter acres(1812)
#485- Kittridge to Ebenezer Perry(1816)
"A"- #465.
James Williams to Dr. Timothy
Kittridge-(1815-1816.)

488-Nickerson
to Nickerson(1816)

489.-John
Nickerson to
Ebenezer Perry
(1816.)

N

Lake   Ontario

EARLY PROPERTY TRANSACTIONS
and
LOT SEVERANCES
in
DOWN-TOWN COBOURG.

Scale 1"= 4Chains.

Canada with the U.E. Loyalists set up circuits and assigned men to visit the settlers. After the year 1800, one of the Methodist circuits extended from the Bay
of Quinte to Yonge Street. The Smiths's Creek Circuit became a separate field
of work in 1805 and the Rev. Thomas Madden was the first stationed minister.
Hull's Corners, on Division Street, North, became the headquarters for the Smith's
Creek Circuit about this time.

The Presbyterians were also active in early settlement times. The first systematic
effort to send Presbyterian ministers to Upper Canada, was made by the Dutch
Reformed Church of the United States. In 1798, the Rev. Robert McDowell was
sent by the Presbytery of Albany, as a missionary to this province. His parish
extended from Elizabethtown, now Brockville to York. He preached and organized
congregations in different places. As the Methodist ministers were not allowed
to celebrate marriages, Mr. McDowell is reported to have celebrated 1,100 marriages prior to 1836 for those who were not members of the Church of England.
The first Presbyterian service in this vicinity was held in the house of Mr. Eldridge
Stanton. (Lot Number 9, Concession I, Hamilton Township). As Mr. Stanton
died in 1812, we can trace Presbyterian services to a time previous to that date.

St. John's Lodge, Number 17, A.F.&A.M., was warranted on October 4, 1801,
and continues to be active to the present time. Free Masonry came to what later
became the Dominion of Canada prior to 1763, when New France became a
British Colony. Masons met in Grand Lodge at Quebec. Afterwards the pioneers,
retired officers and soldiers, the United Empire Loyalists exemplified Masonry
and set up lodges as they had the opportunity.

In this area, even before the Newcastle District was formed in 1802, four lodges
were warranted about the year 1800. Of two of these, United Lodge of Murray,
and Mount Moriah of the Township of Hope, very little is known. North Star
Lodge of the Township of Hamilton, met in what became the Village of Amherst.
Meetings were held in Stile's Hotel. (Note: Lewis Stiles purchased six acres of
land at the South-East corner of Burnham and Elgin Street in 1817, and it was
here his popular hotel stood.) In pioneer times Masonry in and around Cobourg
developed principally under Lodge No. 19 (17), St. John's Lodge.

It is interesting to note some of the names of pioneers who were connected with
Masonry. The list includes: *Caleb Mallory, Mark Burnham, Dr. John Gilchrist,
Barnabus McKeyes, Thomas Ward, Lewis Stiles, John Grover, Manchester Eddy,
John Peters, Joseph J. Losee, Benjamin Ewing, James Norris, Joseph A. Keeler,
Samuel S. McKenning* and others.

In the early years, meetings were held in Governor's Inn, Grafton; at the house
of Caleb Mallory; and at the house of John Kelly, located at the eastern boundary of Hamilton Township, Concession 1.

Lieutenant Governor Simcoe was a planner, a promoter and encouraged the
development of Upper Canada. He employed his best efforts to build up the
population, to establish trade, and the movement of produce to markets, also
to improve conditions. During his tenure of office the settlements were expand-

ing. The action days of the Simcoe regime drifted into inertia days of succeeding Lieutenant Governors. Those who followed Simcoe were of a much different type. Hunter, who replaced Simcoe did not have "the Drive" for increased settlement. The number of new settlers decreased yearly. Those who came to Canada were mostly from the U.S.A. In Europe the Napoleonic Wars were raging with very little emigration from Great Britain to America. The war of 1812-1814 was another factor. All this had its effect on the advancement of the province and Cobourg, in particular, was at a stand-still until the year 1816.

The First Industry

In the meantime, there is one area of local activity we must record. Roger Bates, an early resident reports: "The first saw-mill erected in the neighbourhood was where the present Ontario Mills and Factory stand, and was put up by the father of Colonel McDonald, of Peterborough, in 1803. This was a great boon to the people, who were always in want for a few boards to finish off their shanties."

The land grant to Elias Jones, Jr. in 1797, of Township Lots Numbers 19 and 20, was a valuable one in that the property included a larger creek with a good flow of water, a large estuary that was a safe harbour for small boats, and the higher ground above the creek valley contained a rich, black loam soil. The stream had fish in abundance. Water power was a big potential. The levels of Lake Ontario fluctuated by about five feet over cycles of years, and the high-level water reached well inland to the present day King Street. The old trail crossed the stream at this point where vehicular traffic forded the creek on a shallow limestone bottom.

Some 200 feet upstream from this spot, the first water-power dam was erected possibly as early as the year 1803. Property transactions follow an interesting pattern.

Elias Jones, Jr. owned additional property in Hamilton Township. His wife, née Peggy Harris, received a grant of 200 acres, as a daughter of a U.E. Loyalist father. Jones was active in various pursuits.

In December of 1803, Elias Jones sold his Lot Number 20, in Concession "A" and "B" to John Nugen, all 215 acres, except for 2½ acres on the lake front at the South-East Angle of the lot. It is assumed this small parcel contained the residence of Elias Jones. He also retained his adjoining lot Number 19, until the year 1819. The deed does not mention the price Nugen paid for his purchase. Nugen may have proceeded to erect a dam and build a saw-mill. Further, in December of 1803, John Nugen turns over his newly acquired property to William Carson, his father-in-law, who may have financed the construction of dam and mill. Again no consideration is mentioned in the deed.

The next change is in June of 1806, when William Carson sells out Lot Number 20 to Donald MacDonell, of Kingston, for the sum of 547 Pounds. MacDonell retains the property until September of 1817, when Alexander McDonell, heir

The Jones Creek Development

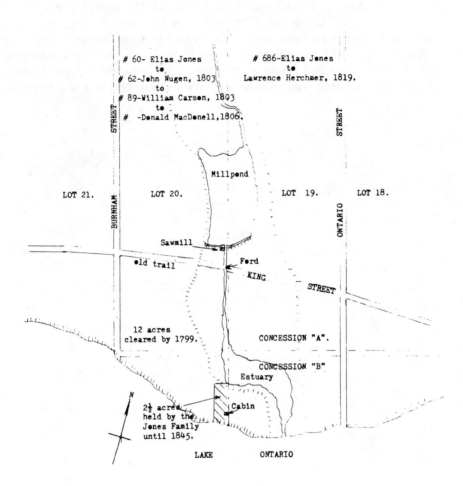

at law of Donald McDonell sells out to Robert Henry, merchant of Montreal and James Bethune, merchant of Kingston, in the amount of 1,500 Pounds. By that time industry had been well established on the stream.

By the year 1816, after the close of hostilities with the United States, and the termination of the Napoleonic Wars in Europe, the core of what later became Cobourg was ready for expansion; industry had been established on the larger creek; the Village of Amherst at the Court House was beginning to take shape, and the Methodists had centered their area activities in Hamilton Township, at what later became Hull's Corners. A new era for the place was beginning.

VII/A NEW ERA BEGINS

Very few settlers came to Upper Canada in the year 1816. Antagonism and a certain amount of enmity towards newcomers from the United States had developed as a result of the recent war. In 1817 a record number of land grants were issued and the movement of immigrants from the United Kingdom had commenced.

In the year 1816, changes made a start in what later became Cobourg. The Nickerson family sold out their property. The 200 acres north of King Street was bought by Mr. John Spencer and the south section went to Mr. Ebenezer Perry. Both of these men were promoters and developers. Elijah Buck arrived earlier and purchased 100 acres from Moses Alley, on the west side of Division Street and north of University Avenue. Other names began to appear as land owners such as Alexander McDonell, Dr. Timothy Kittridge, Jeremiah Lapp, James Williams, John Monjeau, Robert Henry, James Gray Bethune, Henry Ruttan and others in the locality. John Spencer donated four acres of land in 1819 for St. Peter's Episcopal Church, and about this time a post office was established. Cobourg must have a name.

The Naming of Cobourg

The writer is fond of the story as told by Mrs. James Wells, and published in "Home Sketches" of 1874. Mrs. Wells was born near Cobourg in 1803. "As the spot on which the town now stands began to take shape in the form of a little village, the settlers gave it the name of *"Hardscrabble"* by way of a joke on their own hardscrabbling to get along. One of the inhabitants was desirous of having this name changed to *"Buckville"* and built a tavern which he called *"Buckville Tavern"*, and which stood, if we mistake not, where the Toronto Bank now stands. (S.W. corner of King and Division Streets). He had a sign painted and erected on two cedar posts before the door, but the glory of *"Buckville Tavern"* was of short duration, for when the proprietor opened the door on the morning after the erection of this sign, all that remained of it was about a foot and a half of cedar posts, the rest of it having disappeared mysteriously during the night.

"When the first Episcopal Church was built, the steeple was surmounted with a weather cock in the form of a fish, and the village was dubbed "Salmon City". But in time "Hardscrabble", "Buckville" and "Salmon City" gave way to the staid old name of *Cobourg*."

The Methodist Centre to the north of the village became known as 'Hamilton' and the name was also applied to the core village.

The timing of the naming of Cobourg is recorded in the Kingston (Ontario) Chronicle – Volume I, Number 16, Page three and dated 16 April, 1819, in a short news item:

> "At a meeting of the inhabitants of the lower Village of Hamilton, Newcastle District, the following Resolution was read and unanimously adopted:
>
> Resolved, – 'That this village be henceforth called *Cobourg*.'
> Cobourg, 8th April, 1819."

It is interesting to note that Port Hope received its name at a meeting held for the purpose about that time. George Strange Boulton, a young Barrister residing in Port Hope at that time, suggested the name which was unanimously adopted. ("Ye Olden Times, Cobourg World, May 24, 1901-2:2.)

Early Schools

It appears that the first Cobourg school, held in an abandoned stable, was terminated by the year 1813. Elias Jones, School Trustee, in a letter dated 30th of August, 1816, and addressed to the central government, states: "...that in consequence of the great difficulty, for the last three years, in obtaining a teacher adequate to the overseeing the Public School...there has been no public school kept."

It may have been shortly after this letter was written, that a large frame building was erected on the east side of Division Street, nearly opposite the end of Covert Street, and was used as the District School house, also for public meetings and church services. In 1816 the Government passed an Act with respect to schools and contributed funds for maintenance and towards teachers' salaries.

It was about 1817 when steam-boats started to travel on Lake Ontario. The Kingston Chronicle newspaper of May 17, 1819, advertises the time table and ports of call for the steam-boat *Frontenac* under James Mackenzie as Master. The ad gave in detail the various rates for passengers and various articles of freight. The boat was equipped with berths. At Cobourg it was necessary for larger vessels to anchor off shore and convey cargo and passengers to land by Jolly Boat.

In 1820, the Methodists erected their first church building at Hull's Corners, a two-storey structure. For several years previous, this location had a parsonage,

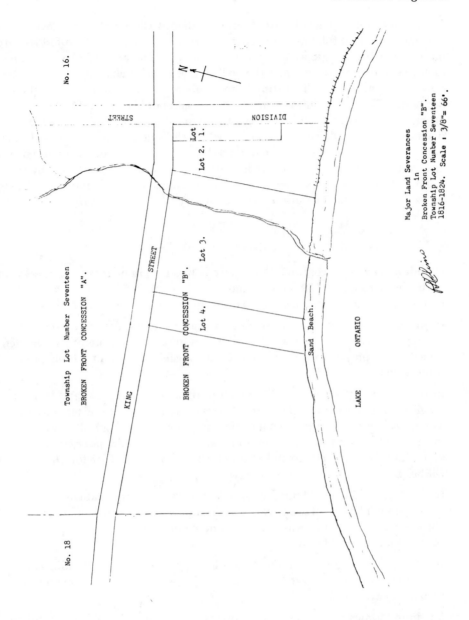

Major Land Severances
in
Broken Front Concession "B".
Township Lot Number Seventeen
1816-1824. Scale : 3/8"= 66'.

a log house, for a centre for use by the Methodist Circuit Riders. There is an interesting item of folklore connected with this early church: "It would require quite a stretch of imagination to conceive of a row of Indian babies each strapped to a board and stood up along the wall in one of our town churches. Yet Mr. Powell informs us that he distinctly remembers seeing such a scene in the old Methodist Church at Hull's Corners. Our Indian population at that time, it appears, were fairly good church attendants. One after another the Squaws would file into church, undo the fastenings by which the board, upon which the Indian baby was strapped and was secured upon their backs, and quietly stand the board and child up against the wall. It is said the Indian infant preserved an air of stolid indifference to its surroundings, and seldom cried no matter how long the sermon." (The Cobourg World, February 21, 1902 - 1:6).

Property Purchases

Hamilton Township continued to receive newcomers in increasing numbers. In 1816, the Census lists 119 families and by 1823 some 243 families were counted by the enumerator. In 1820, the Township population was 1,127.

With the lack of any local newspaper during the 1820's, details of events, happenings and general progress are difficult to obtain. A few items will be mentioned about property ownership and land transfers from information gathered from deeds.

In the year 1818, Alexander McDonell purchased a parcel of land located at the north-west corner of present day Victoria Hall. Here he erected a dwelling. The house remained, and when it came time to erect Victoria Hall, it was moved to the south-east corner of King and Bagot Streets. Years later, it was again moved to William Street, to make room for a fine brick dwelling for Mr. Thomas Gillbard.

In 1819, Elijah Buck sold out the south-west corner of King and Division Streets to Benjamin Throop, of Montreal, a merchant, for 450 Pounds. Throop opened a store on this lot and he was in business here until the year 1838, when he rented his store to Mr. Tremaine.

In one deed, First Street is named Potash Street due to a potash industry located on the west side. George Street was first known as William Street and mentioned in early deeds.

Mr. John Monjeau, who kept a store on the south side of King Street to the west of First Street, became active in purchasing properties both north and south of downtown King Street. In 1820 all his holdings were transferred to *Francois Trudeau*, a Montreal merchant, and Monjeau's name disappears from local records. He possibly went bankrupt. At the same time time Trudeau acquired much land in Cobourg. Moses Alley sold him 50 acres at the north end on Elgin Street, west of Division Street. Through other transactions, Trudeau owned all the land south of King Street, from the small creek westward to Ontario Street,

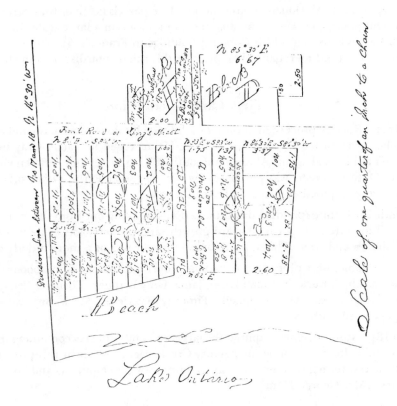

Facsimile of Cobourg's First Plan of Subdivision

Registered the First of October, 1824, as Memorial No. 1163.

Before 1824, individual parcels of land and lots had been marked out in what is today the business section of town.

except for Mr. McDonell's house and lot. Two parcels north of King Street came into his possession. He was an absentee land owner on a large scale. In the year 1824, Trudeau sold all his Cobourg holdings to Francois Antoine LaRocque, also a Montreal merchant. The price of this sale is not disclosed in the deed.

First Land Subdivision

Mr. La Rocque proceeded at once to subdivide his downtown acres and created Cobourg's first plan of land subdivision. He arranged for James Gray Bethune to act as his local agent. All the land south of King Street and between Hibernia and Ontario Streets was purchased by Mr. Ebenezer Perry. Other subdivision lots were disposed of piecemeal over the years.

Until 1824, the expanding downtown core, spreading out from the four corners in all directions, was a haphazard growth, and property lots came in a variety of shapes and sizes. The new subdivision layout was of a more orderly design.

Other names were prominent in various property transactions in Cobourg's core, such as Elijah Buck, Jeremiah Lapp, James Gray Bethune, Ebenezer Perry, James Williams, Alexander McDonell, Timothy Kittridge, Mark Burnham, John Spencer and others.

In 1817, Robert Henry acquired the large west end property containing the dam and mill site on the Jones or Factory Creek. Henry retained this property, all 203 acres, for nearly fourteen years, adding new developments and later selling out to Mr. George Ham.

The Waterfront

The Cobourg Waterfront, with its attractive sand beach, was the stopping-off place for many immigrants en route to the back country. The lakebank was close by to King Street merchants. At Division Street the distance from the lake bank to the south side of King Street was eight chains or 528 feet. At Third Street, eight chains was the measure and at Hibernia Street the distance between the two was eleven chains, all in a short walking distance.

The Reverend Anson Green, D.D., a Methodist Circuit Rider assigned to the local Smith's Creek Circuit writes an interesting account in his memoirs: "When in Cobourg last October, (1824) I saw the beach west of Division Street covered with small white tents filled with Irish immigrants. The Hon. Peter Robinson had been home and brought out a shipload of these people, whom he had landed here. There was no wharf at Cobourg then, and the landing was somewhat difficult. They were to be located in the bush beyond Rice Lake... These white tents presented a beautiful and attractive appearance. They stretched along the sand beach lying between the lake and a forest of small cedars, which covered the worst part of the swampy ground east of Ham's Mills."

The Methodists in Cobourg were increasing. It is on record they held meetings first in the Division Street Common School. In the year 1824, they acquired land and built a small frame chapel at the south-east corner of Division and Chapel Streets. This building was opened in November of 1824, by the Reverend Anson Green.

Up to the year 1825, the growth of the Village of Cobourg was rather slow. By the mid 1820's, the flow of newcomers began to increase, and the increase accelerated each succeeding year. Hard times in Great Britain, following in the wake of the Napoleonic Wars, gave larger numbers the incentive to migrate and to seek a new life in a new land. Slowly but surely the general growth of the Village of Cobourg also started to accelerate. More people took up land and commenced farming in the neighbouring area. Hamilton Township Assessment Rolls report increase from 295 families in 1825 to 396 families in 1830. The Village of Cobourg prospered.

Some New Arrivals

A powerful personality in the person of George Strange Boulton moved to Cobourg from Port Hope in the year 1824. He was a young Barrister at Law, and he had just received the appointment of Registrar of deeds, etc. for Northumberland County. He was a son in a wealthy family, highly placed in provincial political circles. For the remainder of his lengthy life, which ended in 1869, he was active in business affairs and took part in various phases of Cobourg developments. In 1825 he acquired a valuable piece of land in the easterly part of Cobourg and on it erected a large mansion named "Northumberland Hall". It was here he lived out his days.

Three Clench brothers arrived in Cobourg in 1825. They were excellent tradesmen in fine cabinet work. They too contributed to Cobourg life for many years.

Another dynamic person, Henry Ruttan, newly appointed Sheriff for the District, moved to Cobourg from Grafton, and purchased early in 1828, 100 acres to the west of Ontario Street and south of Elgin Street. He erected a very fine home on the north end of his property. A short time later he acquired an additional 92 acres to the south of his first purchase, parts of which were subdivided into town lots and sold piecemeal. Henry Ruttan was an outgoing citizen and contributed both time and talent to various Cobourg enterprizes for many years.

In the year 1828, the Northumberland Agricultural Society was organized at a meeting held in Colborne. The following year, this organization staged their first fair in Colborne. From time to time, in years following, Cobourg was the host to the meetings and fairs held by this organization. Some local men and Hamilton Township farmers took active parts in promoting the welfare of this Society.

Cobourg Harbour

It may have been in the year 1828 when a group of local men decided the time had come for Cobourg to have a landing wharf and a harbour on its waterfront. The central government was approached and permission was asked to organize a joint stock company and to proceed with construction of piers to form a harbour.

For this purpose an Act was passed on the 20th of March, 1829, entitled: "An Act to Improve the Navigation of Lake Ontario, by Authorising the Construction of a Harbour at Cobourg, by a Joint Stock Company." The preamble reads in part as follows:

> "Whereas, the construction of a safe and commodious Harbour at Cobourg, in the District of Newcastle, would manifestly tend to the improvement of that part of this Province, as well as be of great advantage to all persons in any way concerned in the navigation of Lake Ontario;

> "And whereas *Walter Boswell, George Strange Boulton, Benjamin Throop, Charles Perry, Ephraim Powell, James Gray Bethune, John Gilchrist, Ebenezer Perry, Dougald Campbell, Henry Ruttan, Stoddard Bates, Alexander Neil Bethune, Joseph Ash,* and *Archibald Mcdonald,* have petitioned to be by law incorporated for the purpose of effecting the construction of such a harbour by means of a joint stock company; ..."

The Act continued to spell out in detail guide lines for the operation of the Company. The assembly of timber, stone and material for the installation of pier cribs commenced after the passing of the Act. The first stone-filled timber crip was placed in the lake off the shore at the end of Division Street. A space was allowed between the sunken cribs and above water part of the pier was built with a continuous timber formation, capped by heavy plank. A second pier was started from the shore a short distance to the west of Third Street. both piers were aligned towards a convergence point well out in deep water, with the object to close in a safe and commodious harbour. Year by year the piers were advanced into the lake. By the year 1832, ships were able to dock, and the Company collected tolls on goods and produce that passed over their wharf. The amount of revenue increased year by year and the Company was in a position to pay good interest on the investment.

The Cobourg Harbour story is a major one and requires a separate history to give it justice. For this writing we will refer to the subject again later in this presentation. In the year 1850, the Cobourg Harbour company was dissolved, and the Town of Cobourg became the owner of this facility – but at a price!

There is one item of interest to note here. In the summer of 1982, a sewer excavation in the lower end of Division Street uncovered and cut through a part of the first timber crib that was placed in the lake in 1829. The larger squared timbers were sound and showed the marks of the adze. The accumulation of drifting sand, plus the filling in of low ground, today's shoreline is well advanced into the lake in comparison to the shoreline of 1829 in the harbour area.

July 1st, 1984, the Cobourg and District Historical Society erected and unveiled a plaque commemorating the Cobourg Harbour history.

VIII/THE STAR IS BORN

The year 1831 ushers in a second new epoch for Cobourg, in the sense that more detail information is made available to historical writers, due to the launching and the printing of a local weekly newspaper. *Richard Dover Chatterton,* of England, had arrived in Cobourg some time earlier. Under his initiative, guidance, and personal direction, the *Cobourg Star* newspaper was started with the first issue emerging on January 11th, 1831 and has enjoyed a continuous printing to this day. We are greatly indebted to Mr. Chatterton, and succeeding editors, for this newspaper has left for posterity much detail of Cobourg history which would otherwise have been lost and forgotten.

That first number gives us insight to a number of Cobourg citizens of that day. Benjamin Throop advertises rye and corn for sale from the U.S.A. He announces that his distillery (located to the west of First Street) has been enlarged and he sells a superior whiskey. He will also buy wheat and potash. His store has a large assortment of goods. Ebenezer Perry and Dougald Campbell advertise to purchase timber for the Harbour, to be delivered by March 1st. Perry also sells clover seed and cider. Dr. John Gilchrist asks that his accounts be paid. T.M. Jones is the Commissioner for the Canada Company. William H. Draper is a Barrister at Law. T.W. Cleghorn is the proprietor of the Cobourg Hotel, located at the south-east corner of King and Division Streets. Horses are changed here for the York and Kingston stages. F.S. Clench advertises his cabinet and upholstering shop. Other names appear such as Wilson S. Conger; A.B. Carpenter; J.G. Bethune, Postmaster; Elijah Buck wishes to sell his properties; John Bennett; G.M. Boswell and others are all recorded, in that January 11th, 1831 issue. An interesting record!

The Year 1831

The January 18th number of the Cobourg Star advertises Mr. Archibald Fraser,

Amherst, is selling off a quantity of articles and goods by auction.

The February 1st issue has some interesting news. Three petitions have been presented to the House of Assembly praying that the new court house and gaol be located (1) in Cobourg, (2) in Port Hope, and (3) to remain at Amherst. The latter was finally selected for the site.

The Methodists are in the news. A Committee was considering a site and location for their Academy. The places reviewed were York, Cobourg, Colborne, Belleville, Kingston and Brockville. The final choice was for Cobourg by a majority of five to two. Mr. John McCarty was appointed to receive subscriptions. Land for the Academy was donated by Mr. George Spencer.

The year 1831 has recorded other items of interest. In May the Northumberland Agricultural Society held a cattle show and ploughing match in Cobourg, on land owned by Mr. Ebenezer Perry. A new line of stage to Rice Lake was placed in operation for twice a week service. Mr. Peter McCallum arrived in Cobourg and commenced a tailor and furnishing business that later expanded and remained on King Street for 98 years. June 4th was Militia Day in Cobourg with various units taking part in drill and parade exercises. William Weller advertises his stage line to the Carrying Place. Mr. Robert Henry sells out his large property of 203 acres, located in the west end, containing a mill pond, water-powered industries, goods, chattels, farm utensils, etc. to Mr. George Ham, of the Village of Bath, for the sum of 6,000 Pounds. In October the new Court House and Gaol, in a new location was opened at Amherst. The former wooden structure was across Burnham Street opposite to the new one. Perhaps the most important news of the year was the arrival of many new immigrants at the Cobourg waterfront, destined mostly for the Newcastle District. The population of the District reached the figure of 16,500 by late 1831.

The subject of a public market for Cobourg was under discussion at a citizens meeting, held in the District School House in December. A Committee was appointed to search out a site location consisting of Dougald Campbell, L. Church, James Young, J. Helms and G.M. Boswell. This public market matter was raised from time to time, but it took nearly eight years before the market was established.

We wish to present here a definition of a Police Village. Such a village is where police regulations are to be enforced with respect to ladders on roofs, buckets, bakers' and brewers and ashery chimneys, stove-pipes, entering certain places with candles, etc; the lighting of fires in wooden houses, vessels for the carrying of fire, hay, straw; keeping the sale of gun powder, deposit of ashes; quick lime not to be left near wood; the lighting of fires in the streets; charcoal furnaces forbidden within limits; filth, rubbish, etc. These types of regulations apply to within a defined area and are administered by some legal authority. The regulations are mostly for fire prevention in a built-up area, but conditions affecting public health can also be regulated.

The Cobourg and Amherst Fire Company
and
Police Villages of Cobourg and Amherst

Effective January 13, 1832.

The Cobourg Fire Department – Its initial organization

The Editor of the newspaper, *Mr. R.D. Chatterton,* realizing the extreme danger of fire, especially in wooden buildings, and taking note of the formation of a fire department in the Town of York, in an editorial comment, suggested that Cobourg organize a fire department. This idea was published on August 23, 1831.

No action was taken by the inhabitants of Cobourg!

A few months later the Village had a severe fire. A two storey Hotel, located at the north-west corner of King and Division Streets, and erected about the year 1817, took fire at the north end of the building, with a north-east wind blowing. The fire also consumed a second hotel adjacent on King Street. One man nearly lost his life in the blaze. Others lost heavily. With great effort on the part of village inhabitants, the flames were finally subdued.

Immediately the inhabitants called a meeting. A committee was formed, and the District Magistrates were petitioned to officially set up rules and regulations for fire protection and organize fire wardens.

Through the courtesy of the Archives of Ontario, we record the details of the petition and the list of rules to be applied to the Villages of Cobourg and Amherst.

To their Worships the Magistrates of the District of Newcastle in Quarter Sessions assembled.

The Petition of the Inhabitants of the Village of Cobourg Humbly Sheweth

That the want of efficient Regulations in Cases of fire renders the property of your Petitioners liable to severe losses.

That your Petitioners at a public meeting held for the purpose of concerting measures for the preservation of property from fire have determined that the adoption of the rules and regulations annexed to the Petition would be very beneficial in the object your Petitioners have in view. That by a Provincial Act of Parliament passed in the 32d year of the reign of his late Majesty, King George the third, The Magistrates in each District in Quarter Sessions Assembled are authorized to make such orders and regulations for the prevention of accidental fires as to them shall seem meet.

Your Petitioners therefore pray that your Worships will be pleased to Confirm the rules and regulations which they submit for your consideration.

And Your Petitioners will ever pray so.

G.M. Boswell, Secretary for the Petitioners.

The Petition of the Inhabitants of Cobourg to the Quarter Sessions Filed the 13th of January, 1832
T. Ward, Clerk of the Peace

Rules & Regulations made by the Magistrates of the Newcastle District in general Quarter Sessions Assembled for Cobourg and Amherst Fire Company January 11, 1832.

Article 1st. – Four Fire Wardens shall be chosen annually by a majority of the inhabitant householders on the first Tuesday in the month of January in each and every year, at a meeting to be held in the Village of Cobourg, which meeting shall be convened by the Committee of the Fire Company, who are to give three days public notice thereof. The duty of said Fire Wardens shall be to inspect stove pipes, ovens, fire places etc., and to order such removals or alterations as safety may render necessary.

2nd. – the Fire Wardens or any two of them are to attend and make inspection on application to that effect, made by two of the householders.

3d. – The Fire Wardens are to make a quarterly inspection of Stove pipes, etc., Viz: on the first Tuesday in January, April, July, and October in each and every year. A general inspection is to take place forthwith.

4th. – Any person refusing to comply with any order, for removal or alteration, shall, upon complaint made upon Oath by any two of the Fire Wardens, before any one of His Majesty's Justices of the Peace, be fined in a penalty not exceeding the sum of Ten Shillings of Provincial Currency, for every offence, and the continuance of any such nuisance shall be deemed a separate offence.

5th. – The fines to be collected by warrent and sale of the offender's goods in the same way that taxes are now collected.

6th. – The occupant of every Mill, Store, or Merchant Shop, and each two-story house, shall furnish two good leather fire buckets, each to contain not less than three gallons; the occupants of all other houses, store-houses, distilleries, potasheries, breweries, Mechanics Shops, Printing and other offices, *one* each.

7th. – A ladder to be furnished by the occupant of every dwelling.

8th. – Any person required by these regulations to furnish ladders and buckets and not complying within three months after public notice given thereof by the Fire Wardens, shall upon complaint made upon Oath by any two of the Fire Wardens, before any one of His Majesty's Justice of the Peace, be fined in a penalty not exceeding the sum of Ten Shillings for each Bucket, and Five Shillings for each ladder, to be collected in the same manner as directed in Rule 5. But the Magistrate before whom the information is made, shall in his discretion exempt from either of the above named penalties any person who shall make it appear to the satisfaction of the Magistrate that he is unable through poverty to comply with the conditions of this rule.

9th. – That Messers. Church and Conger and any other two persons who may be named by the Committee shall act as Fire Wardens for the present year.

10th. - the Fire Wardens are to act as Treasurers, receive all subscriptions connected with the object of these regulations, and lay an annual statement of the funds they may receive, before a Committee of five persons who are to be designated the *Cobourg* and *Amherst Villages Fire Company,* who are to have the dispositions of said funds.

11th. - That the Committee for the present year shall consist of *Ebenezer Perry; James Gray Bethune; Benjamin Throop; Robert Henry* and *Jas. Radcliffe,* Esquires, and that the Committee shall in each and every subsequent year be chosen in the same manner and form as directed for the election of Fire wardens. The Committee and Fire Wardens shall have full power and authoriety at all fires to order any person present to assist. And any person so ordered and refusing, or neglecting to obey, shall be fined not exceeding the sum of ten shillings, upon information upon oath, made before any one of His Majesty's Justices of the Peace, by any one of the said Committee or Fire Wardens.

12th. - That the limits of the Fire Company shall extend from and including the Honorable Zaccheus Burnham's dwelling house, to Elsworth's Bridge below Cobourg, and also includes half a mile on each side of the main road.

13th. - That each Fire Warden and Members of the Committee shall at all fires, wear a white badge tied around the left arm above the elbow.

14th. - No single building to have more than two Buckets and one ladder unless occupied by two or more families.

15th. - A person to be appointed to sweep chimneys and clean stove pipes which shall be performed at each house once in six weeks. . . Committee to fix the price to be paid by the occupants.

Rules and Regulations for the Cobourg and Amherst Fire Company
Filed January 13, 1832. T. Ward, Clerk of the Peace, W. Falkner, Chairman

With the above regulations becoming active the villages of Cobourg and Amherst became what is know as *Police Villages,* whereby the inhabitants must conform to rules set up by some legal authority, in this case the District Magistrates meeting in Quarter Session. This authority continued until July 1st. 1837, when the new By-Laws of the Incorporated Town of Cobourg came into force. The powers of administration were then transferred from the District Magistrates to the elected Board of Police and the Fire Companies came under the town administration.

The Great Migration

The year 1832 is noted for the massive exodus of emigrants from the United Kingdom to America, to Canada, and many came to find new homes in Upper Canada. Edwin Clarence Guillet, in his book "The Great Migration" tells the story of the movement of thousands across the Atlantic. He describes the conditions of that time; the overcrowding of ships, the privations, the sufferings and the deaths. It is a vivid story. The year 1832, is also noted for the great Asiatic Cholera epidemic which swept across Europe, into Great Britain, moved across the Atlantic, and created much concern in both the United States and the British Provinces in America.

From early Spring, the movement of newcomers up Lake Ontario was heavy. The lake boats were busy with their human cargoes, and many more immigrants landed on the Cobourg wharf.

Cobourg's First Hospital

By June, the Cholera epidemic reached alarming proportions in other places. At Cobourg a local Board of Health was organized, sanitary precautions were taken, and an isolation hospital was set up on the lake bank at the foot of D'Arcy Street. Lake Captains were ordered to take any cholera patients direct to the hospital for a three day quarantine, and not deposit the sick on the Cobourg pier. The Province financed the Cobourg facilities to the amount of 200 Pounds. The Board of Health continued to function through the summer and it was dissolved at a final meeting late in September. The Board reported Cobourg to be in a healthy condition. In total there were sixteen cases of cholera in the Village. Eleven of these persons died and only one case being a resident of the Village. The others were immigrants taken off boats.

The year 1832 also recorded growth and expansion. New merchants arrived and set up shops. There was ample employment and prosperity. The Commercial Bank of the Midland District appointed Mr. Robert Henry to be its Cobourg agent. James Calcutt, Sr. and his family arrived from Ireland, and commenced his famous brewery business. New steam-boats made their appearance on Lake Ontario and competed for trade.

The Steamboat *"Cobourg"*

Late in the fall of 1832, some of Cobourg's citizens decided to build and operate their own steam-boat. A joint stock company was formed, and the following building committee was organized: J.G. Bethune, C. Clarke, E. Perry, B. Throop, Captain C. McIntosh, and W.S. Conger. It was decided to name the new boat *"Cobourg"*. The stock books were opened and preparations went forward. In the winter, a shipyard was set up at the lakefront on the east side of Division Street. Special timber was assembled, service buildings were erected, and on February 25, 1833, the keel was laid. The boat was built under the direction of Captain Charles McIntosh and supervised by Mr. William Hathaway, master builder. In March the Company advertised for thirty shipwrights. The work proceeded and the launching went forward on May 29th. The launching experienced some unforseen difficulties, and four days of effort were expended before the hull was afloat. It was towed to York for installation of boilers and machinery, and the final finishing. The trial runs took place in the late fall and May 1834 found the steamboat *"Cobourg"* in lake service between Niagara and Prescott. It is reported as a very fine boat with excellent appointments. The boat was 152 feet long, 36 feet in breadth, 11 feet in the hold and a burden of 418 tons.

Circumstances placed the majority of ownership stock in the hands of Toronto people, who outvoted the Cobourg owners and took possession of the boat, directing as to where it would serve. The Cobourg merchants had originally planned to use the vessel for their own trade between Cobourg, Genesee, Kingston and Prescott. The Steamboat "Cobourg" saw service on Lake Ontario for quite a number of years.

Cobourg Prospers

The little village of Cobourg moves ahead. The Cobourg Star of May 29, 1833 reports:

"To a visitor the general aspect of our village is one of great prosperity . . . Seven or eight years ago, amidst the wilderness, which it was then, there scarcely stood a log house to mark the future town of Cobourg. Our inhabitants have prodigiously advanced their capital; the surrounding farmers have shared the general prosperity, while the name poverty is scarcely know among us. Stone and brick buildings are superceding the common frame houses; stone bridges are thrown over our streams, and the shops and stores display the rapid accumulation of capital, together with the increase of the common luxuries of life."

This prosperity just did not altogether happen. Behind it all was a lot of hard work of both settlers and townspeople. The merchants were ever busy. They were outgoing, far-seeing and stood to take heavy risks in new ventures. Cobourg merchants and business men were real "pushers" for better things and for improved conditions.

Methodists Build Cobourg's First Sidewalk

In the same editorial of the 29th of May, 1833, the editor makes a witty, interesting comment. Mr. Chatterton was a member of the Church of England. He proceeds:

"Nor will we pass by the excellent, and certainly the necessary side-walk, which the members of the Methodist Church have raised on the road leading to their Chapel. We wish to see the same desire to improve the village, and a like anxiety to render access to their church easy, manifested by the members of the Episcopal Church. We are certain that during this Spring, a more difficult undertaking for a lady could scarcely be imagined, than an attempt to reach our church on foot. We leave this matter to the ladies; if their influence is too weak to induce the gentlemen to correct this crying evil, we despair of our remonstrances having any effect."

The Presbyterians

With reference to local churches, the year 1833 finds St. Peter's Church of England, active and moving forward from strength to strength. The Methodists were well established in their Chapel on Division Street, and their Meeting House at Hull's Corners. The Presbyterians were preparing for the erection of their own house of worship.

From early settlement days, meeting first in private homes, then in the old Court House, and later in shop accomodation on Orange Street, by 1833, the Presbyterians were receiving subscriptions for the erection of their own building. The Reverend Matthew Miller, their pastor, gave leadership. Sheriff Henry Ruttan donated land on the east side of William Street for the site and by early summer, the contract was let to Mr. Archibald Fraser, who had recently erected the New Court House. Within a year, a fine stone building appeared known as *"The Kirk"*. It was dedicated on July 6th, 1834, and the consecration service was conducted by the Reverend Mr. Ketchum, of Belleville.

Citizens' Meetings

Citizens of the young village, especially on long winter's nights, from time to time, would gather in the candle-lit District School House, appoint a chairman and a secretary, and spend the evening discussing local affairs. At this time, the Police Village of Cobourg was still part of Hamilton Township and the Annual Town Meeting system. The government-appointed District Magistrates, meeting in Quarter Sessions, had final say on local politics. Cobourg had its Path Masters, who kept an eye on the conditions of the village streets. Otherwise there was no village organization, and the inhabitants would come together to meet on their own initiative.

One such general meeting was held on Friday evening, the 28th of December, 1832. Much interest was developing in the area to the north of Rice Lake. Town merchants were anxious to tap the trade of that new area. One subject under discussion that evening was the building of a railroad from Cobourg to Rice Lake. Apparently, Mr. F.P. Rubidge had already made a preliminary survey and had found an acceptable route for such a facility. Resolutions were passed and a Committee was appointed with the object of petitioning the Legislature for such a project, was advanced. Interesting!

A second important subject was fully discussed at this same meeting; the idea of incorporating the Village of Cobourg and annexing with it the Village of Amherst. Due to the lateness of Legislature in session, it was decided to postpone any measures in this direction until the next session of the Legislature, when the matter could receive more mature consideration.

A whole year passed by and again the subject of incorporation was brought to the fore. On the evening of Saturday, the 15th of February, 1834, an adjourned meeting of the inhabitants and householders of Cobourg was held in the schoolhouse. Several resolutions were passed spelling out recommended details for the presentation of a petition to the Legislature for incorporation. The new boundaries for the town were also proposed, but leaving out the Village of Amherst.

Two days later, Monday February 17th, a second large meeting was held by another group of citizens, strongly opposed to any incorporation until it is made clear as to the details of the proposed Bill.

The editor of the Cobourg Star, in his February 19th issue, commented in part: "...The advantages of being incorporated must be apparent to everyone, as it is well known that no public improvement can be looked for without. We can have neither markets, sidewalks, lamps, watch, police, nor indeed any public comfort whatsoever, while on the other hand, the only danger of incorporation arises from the possibility of its being invested in too much power." For Cobourg, incorporation had to wait another three years, while other places in the province were incorporated into organized communities.

In November of 1833, the Cobourg Fire Company received its fire pumper from Rochester. Hook and ladder equipment was on order and a new phase of fire protection was in progress, by means of public subscriptions.

The Cobourg Elective Police Bill

The evening of January 7th, 1835, again saw a public meeting in Cobourg numerously attended by the inhabitants of both Cobourg and Amherst, supporting the proposed union of the two villages under the common name of the Town of Cobourg. The resulting petition was presented to the Legislative Assembly that same month. As a result, the Cobourg Elective Police Bill was read for the first time in the House on March 11, 1835. What produced the delay of two years in finalizing and passing this piece of legislation, we are unable to report.

The winter of 1835 is reported in the Cobourg Star as being a very cold one with skating on the open Lake Ontario. The writer also recalls doing the same thing one winter in the 1920's.

In January of 1835, a public meeting was held and discussed several topics of local interest. One of the subjects was the need of a lighthouse for the Cobourg Harbour. A local citizen Mr. John Bennett assumed the task of bulding a high windmill, which was also to serve as a lighthouse. The site of the structure was to the west of Durham Street, and near present Sydenham Street, earlier known as Windmill Street. The windmill was destroyed in early November of 1835, when a severe wind storm completely dismantled the sails.

The Cobourg Railway Company

The Legislature finalized and passed the Act of Incorporation of the Cobourg Railway Company early in 1835. This permitted the Company to proceed with the sale of stock, as specified in the Act. By early June sufficient stock had been subscribed to convene a meeting of the stockholders for the election of Directors. This meeting was advertised and held on the 10th of August. The following is the result of the election and the selection of officers that followed:

President – Hon. Walter Boswell
Secretary – Mr. Alfred Rubidge
Treasurer – Mr. Robert Henry
Directors: Ebenezer Perry, Benjamin Throop, Wilson S. Conger and Kenneth Mackenzie

The Company engaged Mr. Nicol Hugh Baird, recently moved to Cobourg from Montreal, and ordered him to proceed at once to make a detailed survey for the route of the railway. He was assisted by Mr. F.P. Rubidge, who had explored the route earlier. The survey was completed that August, and a direct route, with satisfactory grades, was laid out from Cobourg to Rice Lake. The Directors were pleased with the economic features of the proposed railway, but there was a delay in starting actual construction.

In May of 1836, another Act of the Legislature was passed to extend the time for the commencement of construction. Another Annual Meeting of Stockholders took place on July 4th, 1836, and the Directors were re-elected. Next, the Directors applied to the Legislature for a loan of 10,000 Pounds. This was authorized in February of 1837. At a meeting on March 13, additional stock was subscribed, and a resolution was passed to proceed with construction without delay. For some reason there was delay. At a June meeting the names G.S. Boswell and G.M. Boswell were added to the Directorate. The first payment of 10% of the stock subscribed was called for July the First, 1837. Then on June the 21st, the following notice appeared in the Cobourg Star:

"The Directors of the Cobourg Railroad Company, not deeming it expedient in the present embarrassed state of the country, to press for payment of stock; do hereby give further notice that the payment of the first instalment...is for the present postponed."

It appears difficult economic times had suddenly come upon the country. Money markets dried up, political turbulence and the upcoming rebellion were factors that affected many things in general and the Cobourg Railway Company in particular. Directors were again elected in 1838, and the first payment of 10% of stock was again called for August 15, 1838. Construction did not become a reality, and the Company became defunct. What happened to the 10,000 Pound loan and the first payment of 10% of the stock, we do not know. Probably that money was not forthcoming. Construction was delayed until the 1850's.

Clergy Reserves

Troublesome times were developing in Upper Canada, by 1836. The Lieutenant-Governor, through his appointed Executive Council, and the large Family

L A K E

Line of COBOURG-RICE LAKE Railway
as surveyed in 1835. ++++++++++++

(Marked out on a 1957 map.)

Compact group, controlled developments, and the appropriations of money. The simple settlement days had long since passed, and the population was rapidly increasing, demanding new solutions. There were a number of grievances such as poor roads, the struggle for common schools, and especially the demand that the Legislative Council be elected by the people. The Reform Party attacked the actions of the Family Compact group. The Clergy Reserves issue flared up. The giving of Crown lands to a favoured few, and the attempt to establish the Church of England by Strachan and his followers provoked many people.

Sir John Colborne, in his last important act before leaving the country, had set up fifty-seven Rectories as endowments for Anglican Clergymen. Of these, forty-four were established by writ, and the Cobourg Rectory being one of them, receiving a grant of some 371 acres. Part of this land was in Cobourg.

Township Lot Number 15, to the south of King Street and west of D'Arcy Street was subdivided into streets and town lots by the Crown. A portion of these lots were granted to the local Rectory. Also the west quarter of Lot number 15, between King and Elgin Streets consisting of 50 Acres. This portion of Cobourg became known as the Glebe lands.

The Methodists and the Presbyterians strongly opposed the attempt to establish the Anglican Church in Canada. The Cobourg Presbyterians, in early March of 1837, held a largely attended meeting in the local school house, and passed resolutions against the move.

In April, 1837, delegates from Upper Canada Presbyterian Churches converged and convened in Cobourg for four days, in protest of the movement toward Church establishment. One of the resolutions passed by this church group follows:

> "Lieutenant-Governor, Sir John Colborne, did unwisely and endow 57 Rectories in this Province, which had never before been acted upon, etc., thereby giving clergymen of the Church of England jurisdiction over the members of the Church of Scotland, and over those other denominations. . .etc. . . .thereby weakened the Government in the views of a lot of the inhabitants."

An Address was also sent to the King from this meeting.

Finally there was a reconciliation, and the Presbyterians and other groups received benefits from the sale of Clergy Reserves land.

IX/AGAIN, INCORPORATION OF COBOURG

The subject of incorporating the Village of Cobourg and raising it to town status again surfaced. Apparently there was controversy over the setting of boundaries for the new town, and in February, 1836, two petitions were delivered to the Legislature. One was headed by George Ham and eighty others, freeholders and householders of the Village of Cobourg, protesting incorporation. The other petition was headed by Ebenezer Perry and forty others praying for incorporation and an elective Police in Cobourg. The response was to give the Bill a second reading. In late March, the Cobourg Incorporation Bill was read a third time, but the passing of it was delayed.

The months rolled by and no action was taken to finally pass the legislation. On December 2, 1836, a meeting was held in the Common School House for "the considering the propriety of incorporating the town." Mr. Ebenezer Perry was appointed to the chair. The Cobourg Star of December 7, 1836 reports: "After a number of resolutions were passed, deprecating the annexation of Amherst, and extension of the present limits as proposed in the former petition for an Act of Incorporation, Messers A.A. Burnham, A. Jeffrey, and George Ham, were appointed a committee to draft a petition to both Houses of the Legislature, in accordance with the spirit of the resolutions at the meeting."

Apparently this final approach to the Legislature produced results. "The Act to Establish a Police in the Town of Cobourg, and to Define the Limits of the said Town" was passed on March 4th, 1837. This Act set the necessary machinery in motion to finalize years of debate and to establish the raising of the Town.

Some local historians of past years have conveyed the impression that Cobourg remained a village until the year 1850, and the term "Police Village" has been applied. Unfortunately this mistaken impression has persisted to the present time. A "Police Village" refers to a designated built-up area to which certain rules and fire prevention regulations, are to be followed by the householders. Some legal authority applies and supervises the rules and regulations. Cobourg became a Police Village on January 13, 1832, when the fire department was first organized and a series of fire rules and regulations came into force, authorized and supervised under the District Magistrates meeting in Quarter Sessions.

The term "Police", with reference to a Board of Police may require some clarification. A definition from a large dictionary is:

> "A judicial and executive system in accordance with which a town, city, or district is governed; that system of internal regulation dealing with the enforcement of law, the prevention of crime, and the preservation of rights, order, and health; public order; that which concerns the order of the community."

There is a big difference between a "Police Village" and a "town governed by a Board of Police." It is our plan to reproduce Cobourg's Act of Incorporation in order that the readers can fully understand.

Statutes of Upper Canada. Local and Private Acts
7th Wm. IV. Chap. 42
AN ACT to establish a Police in the Town of Cobourg, and to define the limits of the said Town

(Passed 4th March, 1837)

Preamble

Whereas from the great increase of population of the town of Cobourg, in the Newcastle District, it is necessary to make further provision than by law exists for the internal regulation thereof: *Be it therefore enacted* by the King's most Excellent Majesty, by and with the advice and consent of the Legislative Council and Assembly of the Province of Upper Canada, constituted and assembled by virtue of land under the authority of an Act passed in the Parliament of Great Britain, intituled, "An Act to repeal certain parts of an Act passed in the fourteenth year of His Majesty's reign, intituled 'An Act of making more effectual provision for the Government of the Province of Quebec, in North America,' and to make further provision for the Government of the said Province," and by the authority of the same, That there shall be in the said town a Board of Police, to be composed and constituted in the manner hereinafter described; which shall be and is hereby declared to be a body corporate and politic, in fact and in law, by the name of the "President and Board of Police of Cobourg;" and by that name they and their successors may have perpetual succession, and be capable of suing and being sued, pleading and being impleaded, in all Courts, and in all actions, causes and complaints whatsoever; and may have a common seal, and may alter the same at pleasure; and shall be in law capable of purchasing, holding and conveying, any estate, real or personal, for the uses of the said town.

1. *Board of Police constituted in Cobourg as a body corporate.*

II. *And be it further enacted by the authority aforesaid,* That the said town
of Cobourg shall be comprised within the following limits or boundaries,   *1*
that is to say: commencing on the Lake shore, at the south-east angle of
lot number fourteen, in concession B; thence north, sixteen degrees west,
to the centre of the first concession; thence south, seventy-four degrees west,
to the centre of lot number twenty-one, in said concession; thence south,
sixteen degrees east, to the Lake shore; thence along the water's edge to
the place of beginning.

1. *Limits of the town of Cobourg.*

III. *And be it further enacted by the authority aforesaid,* That for the purpose of electing the members of the said Corporation, the said town shall   *1*
be divided into three wards, in the following manner, that is to say: that
part of the town of Cobourg south of King-street shall compose the south   *2*
ward, all that part of the town east of the centre of the street between lots
number sixteen and seventeen, and north of King-street, shall compose   *3*
the east ward, and all that part of the town west of the centre of the street
between lots number sixteen and seventeen, and north of King-street,   *4*
shall compose the west ward.

1. *Town divided into three wards; 2. South ward; 3. East ward; 4. West Ward.*

IV. *And be it further enacted by the authority aforesaid,* That the east
and west wards shall each elect annually two persons, and the south ward   *1*
one person, annually, to be members of the said Corporation, from among   *2*
the inhabitants of the said town, who being subjects of His Majesty shall   *3*
be freeholders therein to the assessed value of sixty pounds; and that the
persons entitled to vote at the election of either of the said wards shall be
subjects of His Majesty, and male inhabitant householders, resident   *4*
within such ward, who shall severally be possessed for their own use and
benefit of a dwelling-house and lot of ground within the ward in which
they shall so vote, such dwelling-house being by them held in freehold;
or who, at the time of such election, shall bona fide have paid, within one
year next before the election, one years rent for the dwelling-house or
dwelling-houses (if they shall within one year have changed their place of
residence, within the said ward in which they shall have resided), at the
rate of ten pounds per annum, or upwards.

1. *East and West wards to elect two members; 2. South ward to elect one; 3. Qualifications of
candidates; 4. Qualifications of voters.*

V. *And be it further enacted by the authority aforesaid,* That the first   *1*
election of members of the said Corporation shall be holden on the first
Monday in the month of June next, at some place within each ward respectively, to be appointed by the Sheriff of the District of Newcastle, who   *2*
shall give public notice thereof at least six days before the said election;
and who shall preside at the said election for one of the said wards,   *3*
and the Deputy Sheriff and High Constable, or some other person authorised

by the said Sherriff shall preside at the first election of the other wards, and shall declare the persons in such other wards, who shall have the greatest number of votes, to be duly elected members of the said Corporation; and shall give notice thereof to the persons so elected in the said wards as   *4*
members of the said Corporation, within six days after such election.

1. *First election; 2. Notice thereof; 3. Who to preside; 4. Notice to party elected.*

VI. *And be it further enacted by the authority aforesaid,* That the members of the said Corporation, so chosen, shall serve until the first Monday   *1*
of June in the next year, and until a new Board shall be chosen and formed as herinafter mentioned; and that on the first Monday of June in each   *2*
year an election shall be holden for each ward in the said town, for a member of the said Corporation, before the Bailiff of such ward, who shall be   *3*
appointed from time to time by the said Corporation, and who shall appoint the place for holding the said election, and shall give notice thereof,   *4*
and proceed in all respects as the Sheriff is required to do at and after the first election to be holden as aforesaid.

1. *Members to serve till first Monday in June 1838; 2. Elections to be on the first Monday in June; 3. Before the Bailiff of the ward; 4. Notice.*

VII. *And be it further enacted by the authority aforesaid,* That before any person shall proceed to hold an election under this Act he shall take the   *1*
following oath, which any Justice of the Peace for the District of Newcastle is hereby authorised to administer: — "I do solemnly swear, that I will faithfully and impartially, to the best of my ability, discharge the duty of presiding officer at the election which I am about to hold, for a member of the Board of Police of the town of Cobourg — So help me God."

1. *Oath to be taken by presiding officer at elections.*

VIII. *And be it further enacted by the authority aforesaid,* That the officer presiding at any election under this Act shall have authority, and he is hereby required, at the request of any person qualified to vote at such an election,   *1*
to examine an oath, or affirmation (when the party is allowed to affirm,) any candidate for the office of member of the said Corporation respecting his qualification to be elected to the said office; and shall also have authority, and is hereby required upon such request aforesaid, to examine upon oath, or affirmation, (when the party is allowed to affirm,) any person tendering his vote at any election respecting his right to vote; and that the oath to be administered for either of the said purposes shall and may be in the following form: — "You shall true answer make to all such questions as the officer presiding at this election shall put to you, respecting your qualification to be elected at this election, or respecting your qualification to vote at this election, (as the case may be,) — So help you God." And that the affirmation to be taken shall be in the common form of an affirmation to the same effect.

1. *Presiding officer at election may examine parties on oath, as to qualifications as candidate or as voter.*

IX. *And be it further enacted by the authority aforesaid,* That if any person, being examined upon oath or affirmation under this Act, in regard *1* to his qualification to vote or to be elected, shall wilfully forswear himself, he shall be deemed guilty of wilful and corrupt perjury, and on conviction thereof shall suffer as in other cases of wilful and corrupt perjury.

1. *False swearing perjury.*

X. *And be it further enacted by the authority aforesaid,* That if the election of any member of the Board of Police aforesaid shall be complained of, *1* either on the ground of want of qualifications in the person returned, or on the ground that such person had not a majority of legal votes at such election, it shall be the duty of the Sheriff, after the first elections take place under this Act, upon receiving, within forty-eight hours after the termination of the election, a written requisition signed by any three inhabitants of the town having a right to vote at such election, to appoint a time and place within the town or ward for which the election was held for entering into a scrutiny of the matters complained of, and that such *2* time shall be within six days after the election; and the Sheriff shall have the power to summon witnesses, and to take evidence on oath respecting *3* the matters to be inquired into, and shall determine upon the validity of the election or return as shall appear to him to be right according to the evidence; and in case an election shall be declared void, but it shall not appear proper to the Sheriff for any cause to amend the return, by substituting the name of any other person as entitled to have been returned at such election, then he shall, after giving eight days notice thereof, hold a *4* new election for a member to serve according to this Act; and that if after any election to be holden after a Board of Police under this Act shall have been completely organized, a requisition, signed as aforesaid, shall, within forty-eight hours after the termination of such election, be served upon the President or any other member of the Corporation, it shall be lawful for the said Corporation, and they are hereby required, to appoint a time for entering upon a scrutiny of the matters complained of, at any place *6* within the said town, which time shall be within six days after the election; and the Corporation, or such member or members thereof as shall not be individually concerned in the questions to be determined, shall have power to summon witnesses, and to take evidence on oath respecting the *7* matters to be inquired into, and shall determine upon the validity of the election or return as shall appear to be right, according to the evidence; and in case an election shall be declared void, but it shall not appear proper for any cause to amend the return by substituting the name of any other person as entitled to have been returned at such election, then the Corporation shall issue their precept for a new election, as in other cases under *8* this Act.

1. *Proceedings where any return is contested, at the first election; 2. Scrutiny; 3. Summoning witnesses; 4. New election in certain cases; 5. Mode of trial of contested return, on subsequent elections; 6. Scrutiny; 7. Witnesses to be summoned; 8. New election.*

XI. *And be it further enacted by the authority aforesaid,* That before the Sheriff, or any member of the Corporation, shall enter upon any such trial or scrutiny, as aforesaid, he shall take an oath in the following form, before some one of the Justices of the Peace for the District of Newcastle, that is to say:— "I do solemnly swear, that I will truly and impartially, to the best of my judgment, try and determine the merits of the complaint against the election of A.B.—So help me God."

1. Oath to be taken before trial of contested election.

XII. *And be it further enacted by the authority aforesaid,* That any witness who, being duly summoned to attend upon such trial or scrutiny, shall wilfully neglect or refuse to attend upon such trial or scrutiny, shall upon conviction before any one of His Majesty's Justices of the Peace for the District of Newcastle, having been duly summoned to answer such complaint, be liable to be imprisoned, on the commitment of such Justice, in the common Gaol of the District, for a time not exceeding one month.

1. Penalty for witnesses refusing to attend.

XIII. *And be it further enacted by the authority aforesaid,* That the person presiding at any such election shall give public notice, immediately upon declaring the result of the election, of the time and place at which the members of the Corporation are first to meet, which meeting shall be within six days after the election, and at some place within the said town.

1. Notice of meeting of Corporation to be given.

XIV. *And be it further enacted by the authority aforesaid,* That the said five members elected as aforesaid shall, within ten days after their election, appoint one of their number President; and the said President and members shall form the said Corporation, and shall hold their office until the first Monday in June in the ensuing year, and until the election and formation of the new Board.

1. President to be chosen.

XV. *And be it further enacted by the authority aforesaid,* That if either of the members elected as aforesaid, after notice thereof, shall neglect or refuse for ten days to take the oath of office hereinafter contained, which any of the said members so to be elected as aforesaid is hereby authorized to administer to the others, he shall for such neglect or refusal, forfeit the sum of ten pounds, to be recovered, with costs, by information before any Justice of the Peace, who is authorised to proceed in the same manner as hereinafter is provided for the recovery of any penalty for the trangression of any order or regulation of the said Corporation: *Provided* that no person having been elected a member of the said Corporation, without his knowledge or consent, shall be subject to the penalty herein-before stated, for his refusal to act as a member of the said Corporation.

1. Penalty for members refusing to take the oaths of office; 2. Exception.

XVI. *And be it further enacted by the authority aforesaid,* That in case

it shall at any time happen that a vacancy occurs among the members 1
of the said Corporation, by neglect or refusal to take the oath of office
hereinafter contained, within the time herein-before limited, or by death,
removal from the town, or from any other cause, the Corporation shall
issue a precept to the Bailiff of the ward to hold an election for such ward
of said town, giving notice of the time and place of holding the said election; and the member so elected shall hold his office until the next annual
election, or until another is chosen in his place.

1. How vacancies to be filled up.

XVII. *And be it further enacted by the authority aforesaid,* That in case 1
it shall at any time happen that an election of members of the said Corporation shall not be made on any day, when pursuant to this Act it ought
to have been made, the said Corporation shall not for that cause be deemed
to be dissolved, but it shall and may be lawful on any other day, to hold
and make an election of members, in such manner as shall have been regulated by the laws and ordinances of the said Corporation.

1. Corporation not dissolved by reason of default in making an election.

XVIII. *And be it further enacted by the authority aforesaid,* That it shall
and may be lawful for the said Corporation, from time to time to establish 1
such ordinances, by-laws and regulations, for the said town, as they may
think reasonable; to regulate victualling-houses and ordinaries where 2
fruit and victuals shall be sold; to regulate the weighing of hay — measuring 3
of wood; to regulate carts and carmen; to regulate slaughter houses; to 4, 5
to prevent firing of any guns, muskets, pistols, squibs, and fire-balls, or 6
injuring or destroying trees, planted or growing for shade or ornament 7
in the said town; to prevent the pulling down or defacing of any sign-boards; 8
or inscribing or drawing any indecent words, or figures or pictures, on 9
any building, wall, fence, or other public place; and generally to prevent
vice and preserve good order in the said town; to enter into and examine
all dwelling-houses, ware-houses, shops, yards, and out-houses, to ascertain 10
whether any such places are in a dangerous state with respect to fires, and
to direct them to be put in a safe and secure condition; to appoint fire- 11
wardens and fire engineers; to appoint and remove fire-men; to make such
rules and by-laws as may be thought expedient for the conduct of such 12
fire companies as may be raised with the sanction of the said Corporation;
to compel any person to aid in the extinguishment of any fire; to require
the inhabitants to provide and keep fire-buckets and scuttles and ladders 13
to their houses; to stop, or authorise any other person to stop, any one riding or driving immoderately in any street, or riding or driving on any 14
side-walk, and to inflict fines for any such offence; to regulate the assize 15
of bread; to prevent and abate, and remove any nuisances; to restrain and 16
prevent any horses, cattle or swine, from running at large; to prevent 17
and remove encroachments in any streets; and to make such rules and regulations for the improvement, order and good government, of the said town, 18

as the said Corporation may deem expedient, the same not being repugnant to the laws of this Province, except in so far as the same may be virtually repealed by this Act; and to enforce the due observance thereof, by *19* inflicting penalties on any person for the violation of any by-law or ordinance of the said Corporation, not exceeding one pound ten shillings; and to fix upon and to appoint such days and hours for the purpose of selling butchers' meat, butter, eggs, poultry, fish and vegetables, and to make such other orders and regulations relative thereto as they shall deem expedient.

1. Corporation may make by-laws, 2. Victualling houses, 3. Hay, Wood, & c., 4. Carts, 5. Slaughter houses, 6. Fire arms and fire works, 7. Destroying trees, 8. Defacing sign boards, 9. Indecency, 10. To examine houses, & c., 11. Fire wardens, 12. Fire Companies, 13. Fire buckets and ladders, 14. Furious driving, 15. Assize of bread, 16. Nuisances, 17. Cattle running at large, 18. General rules, 19. Penalties.

XIX. *And be it further enacted by the authority aforesaid,* That any rule or regulation of the said Corporation, for the infraction of which any penalty *1* is inflicted, before it shall have any effect, shall be published in one or more of the newspapers of the said town; and that in like manner shall be published, in each and every year, before the annual election, an account of all moneys received and in the treasury, and the amount expended, and for what purpose.

1. Rules and regulations, and money accounts to be published.

XX. *And be it further enacted by the authority aforesaid,* That for the purpose of raising a fund to provide for purchasing any real estate for the *1* use of the said town, to procure fire-engines, aqueducts and a supply of pure and wholesome water; for lighting, paving, flagging and repairing the streets, and for all other purposes deemed expedient and necessary by the said Corporation for the welfare and improvement of the said town, it shall and may be lawful for the said Corporation to lay an assessment annually upon the persons rated or liable to be rated upon any assessment for property in the said town, not exceeding three pence in the pound, *2* exclusive of the sum such persons may be rated for upon any other assessments of this Province; and it shall be the duty of the Clerk of the Peace of the said District, to select from a general assessment of the township of *3* Hamilton, a list or assessment of the ratable property that every person owns or possesses in the said town, and lay the same before the Corporation annually, upon its organization after every general election.

1. Corporation may impose an assessment, 2. Limitation, 3. Clerk of the Peace to make assessment roll.

XXI. *And be it further enacted by the authority aforesaid,* That every town lot in the said town of Cobourg shall be rated upon the assessment roll *1* at twenty-five pounds, and that every lot or portion of a lot on which a house shall be built, shall be deemed and taken to be a town lot.

1. Town lots, how rated.

XXII. *And be it further enacted by the authority aforesaid,* That if any person shall refuse to pay the sum or rate for which he or she stands rated, as aforesaid, for the space of ten days after demand duly made of the same by the Collector, to be appointed by the Corporation for that purpose, the said Collector shall, and he is hereby required to levy the same, by distress and sale of the goods and chattels of the person so neglecting or refusing to pay, after having obtained a warrant for that purpose from some one of His Majesty's Justices of the Peace, who is hereby authorised to grant the same, upon information made on oath before him of the neglect or refusal to pay the said assessment, and to render the overplus, if any there shall be over and above the said rate, to the owner thereof, after deducting the legal charges of the distress and sale.

1. If rates unpaid, Collector may levy same by distress; 2. Warrant.

XXIII. *And be it further enacted by the authority aforesaid,* That the said Corporation may from time to time appoint, and at their discretion remove and re-appoint, a Surveyor of streets for the said town, a Clerk and three Assessors, a Bailiff or Bailiffs, a Collector or Collectors, a Treasurer, and as many and such other officers as they may require, and assign the duty or services to be performed by each, with such salaries and allowances as to them may seem meet, and may take such reasonable security for the due performance of the duties assigned to any officer or servant, as they shall think proper.

1. Corporation may appoint certain officers, 2. Salaries, 3. Security.

XXIV. *And be it further enacted by the authority aforesaid,* That if any person shall transgress the orders or regulations made by the said Corporation, under the authority of this Act, such person shall, for every such offence, forfeit the sum which in every such order, rule, or regulation shall be specified, with costs, to be recovered by information before the said Corporation, to be levied of the goods and chattels of such offender; and in default of such goods and chattels, the offender shall be liable to be committed to the common Gaol of the District, for a time not exceeding one month, in the discretion of the said Corporation, before whom such offender shall be convicted; and that no person shall be deemed an incompetent witness upon any information under this Act, by reason of his being an inhabitant of the said town of Cobourg: *Provided always* that the information and complaint for the breach of any orders or regulations of the said Corporation, shall be made within fifteen days of the time when the offence was committed.

1. Penalty for transgressing rules and regulations, 2. How recovered, 3. Commitment, 4. Witnesses, 5. Limitation of informations.

XXV. *And be it further enacted by the authority aforesaid,* That all penalties recovered under the provisions of this Act shall be paid into the treasury of the said Corporation, and applied in the same manner as other moneys coming into the treasury may be applied for the public uses of the said town.

1. Application of penalties.

XXVI. *And be it further enacted by the authority aforesaid,* That the said Corporation shall and may, in the said town of Cobourg, perform all the functions, and exercise the authority now by law given to the Board of Police in other Police towns within this Province, with respect to making or amending any street, or highway or road within the said town: *Provided always,* that it shall not be lawful for the said Board of Police to lay out, open or establish any new street which might interfere with the powers conferred upon the Cobourg Harbour Company, by the third clause of an Act passed in the tenth year of the reign of His late Majesty George the Fourth, intituled, "An Act to improve the navigation of Lake Ontario, by authorising the construction of a harbour at Cobourg, by a Joint Stock Company."

1. Authority of other Boards of Police, respecting roads, extended to this Corporation, 2. Not to interfere with Harbour Company.

XXVII. *And be it further enacted by the authority aforesaid,* That it shall and may be lawful for the said Corporation to fix upon a site for a market in the said town, and to enter into and make such arrangement or agreements in behalf of the said town for the purchase of such site, as to them, or a majority of them, appear just and reasonable; and the said Corporation shall give at least six weeks notice in the newspapers published in the said town of Cobourg, of the site intended for such market; and if any objection, in writing, to such site shall, within the period of six weeks, be presented or declared to the said Corporation, or any member thereof, signed by twelve persons entitled to vote within the said town, a public meeting of the inhabitants shall be called, and a time and place for such meeting shall be fixed by the said Corporation who shall give at least six days notice thereof; and a majority of the persons present at such meeting, entitled to vote under this Act, shall decide whether such proposed site shall be confirmed or not; and the President of such Corporation shall preside at such meeting, and conduct the proceedings thereof; and that when the site for the said market shall be confirmed, or in case of its being rejected, then when any other site which may be afterwards proposed shall be agreed to, or if objected to in like manner, shall be confirmed, such site shall be the market-place of the said town, any thing herein contained to the contrary in any wise not withstanding.

1. Market, 2. Purchase of site, 3. Notice, 4. In case of objection, public meeting to be held, 5. Majority to decide on site, 6. Site finally agreed to shall be the market place.

XXVIII. *And be it further enacted by the authority aforesaid,* That it shall and may be lawful for the said Corporation to borrow the sum of one thousand pounds, of or from any person or persons, body politic or corporate, willing to lend the same, for the purpose of building a market house, and for purchasing one or more fire-engine or fire-engines, as may be deemed necessary, and to provide some fit and proper place where the same may be kept.

1. Corporations authorized to borrow £1000; 2. For what purposes.

XXIX. *And be it further enacted by the authority aforesaid,* That the Corporation shall set apart so much of the assessments as are authorised *1* by this Act to be raised for the use of the said town, as will be sufficient to pay the yearly interest of the said sum of one thousand pounds, and to liquidate the principal in a term not longer than ten years from and after the time such loan shall have been made.

1. Portion of yearly assessments to be set aside for payment of interest, and principal, within ten years.

XXX. *And be it further enacted by the authority aforesaid,* That in case an equality of votes shall happen at any election for members of the said *1* Corporation in any of the said wards, it shall and may be lawful for the person presiding at the said election to give a casting vote, and he shall not be required to be possessed of the qualifications necessary to enable him to vote at the said election for the said wards, respectively.

1. In case of equality at an election of members of the Corporation, the Presiding Officer may give a casting vote.

FORM OF OATH

I, A.B. do swear, that I will faithfully discharge the duties of a member of the Police of the Town of Cobourg, to the best of my skill and knowledge. So help me God.

The First Town Election

The editor of the Cobourg Star was strangely silent about the incorporation of the town, and the upcoming election for members of the Board of Police. There had been a severe controversy for over four years. Further, provincial elections were severe and sometimes bloody affairs between the two political parties. The year 1837 was not a quiet time with the rebellion breaking out a few months later. The town election was a new venture, and rather than stir up animosity and party strife, the editor may have refrained from comment. A peaceful procedure was desired.

The following two notices appeared in the Cobourg Star on May 24th, 1837:

"*Notice – The Police Election* for the Town of Cobourg, will be held on the first Monday in June next, as the Law directs.

That for the South Ward will be held at *Brown's Inn.*
for the East Ward at *Wilder's Inn.*

for the West Ward at *Battell's Inn.*

All commence at the hour of Ten O'Clock, A.M.

H. Ruttan, Sheriff, N.D.
Sheriff's Office, Cobourg,
May 22, 1837"

"To the Electors of the South Ward of the Town of Cobourg."

"Gentlemen: – Having been instrumental in procuring the Act of Incorporation, which I consider will be productive of advantage to our town, and having in consequence of the great interest I have in its prosperity, been solicited to become a candidate for one of the members of the corporation, I have consented to do so. If you therefore think I can be of service in framing rules and regulations for the government of the town, I solicit your votes at the election, which takes place on the 5th of June; and if elected, I shall endeavour to do all the good I can for the common interest of our town.

"In regard to the Market, gentlemen, I must inform you that no situation can be established for the erection, without the concurrence of the majority of the electors of the town, as the Corporation have no power by the Act to establish a Market contrary to their wishes.

I am, Gentlemen,
Your faithful servant,

"May 22nd, 1837."　　　　　　　　　　　　　　*G.S. Boulton"*

The above election card was the only one to appear in the Cobourg Star. In fact the newspaper gave no list of candidates in the various wards. The only comment is as follows:

> "The first election of officers for the Cobourg Police will take place in this town on Monday next, simultaneously, at the respective inns of Messers Wilder, Brown, and Battell - commencing at ten o'clock precisely."

> "From a perusal of the Act of Incorporation (which has been published by us during the week, and may be had at the Star Office - price three pence) it will be seen that the punctual attendance at the polls, in order to secure the return of an effective and useful Board, is of some importance."

- The Cobourg Star, May 31st, 1837

The results of the election, as reported by the local newspaper follows:

> "The Election for the members of the Corporation, under the present law incorporating this town, took place on Monday last, pursuant to notice, when the following gentlemen were elected, viz:-

E. Perry, Esq.

George Ham　　　　*Andrew Jeffrey*
W.S. Conger　　　　*William Weller*

- The Cobourg Star, June 7th, 1837

The elected members at their first meeting, elected *Ebenezer Perry* as President.

The next item of news connected with the Town of Cobourg is as follows:

The First Cobourg By-Laws
Effective July 1st, 1837

"The Cobourg Board of Police have just published a code of excellent By-Laws for the better regulation of the town. They are extremely well conceived, and require only to be as well administered to produce the happiest effects in our community. As such we shall have much pleasure in extending their circulation by copying them into our next week's Star.

The Cobourg Star, July 5, 1837

General Rules

Regulations and By-Laws,
Of the Board of Police for the town of Cobourg, to become in full force on the first day of July next. (July 1st, 1837).

Be it enacted, by the President, and members of the Board of Police for the Town of Cobourg, that on and after the first of July next, any person who shall be guilty of any of the offences herein mentioned, shall be subjected to the penalties hereinafter prescribed. To Wit:

1st. Any persons who shall on Sundays do any servile work or Labour, (works of piety, charity, and necessity excepted), or buy, sell or show forth, or expose for sale any goods, wares or merchandise, or any other thing, shall forfeit a sum not exceeding thirty shillings for such offence at the discretion of the magistrates convicting.

2nd. That any person or persons firing any musket, pistol, squib, or fireballs within 200 yards of any house or other building in the Town shall be liable to a fine of not less than two shillings and six pence.

3d. That any person or persons bathing within one quarter of a mile of any house within the limits of the town, after sunrise in the morning or before twilight in the evening, shall be liable to be fined at the discretion of the Board; not to exceed ten shillings.

4th. That any person or persons seen shooting or making use of guns or either fire arms, fishing or skating on the Sabbath, within the limits of this Town, shall, upon conviction, pay a fine of not less than two shillings and six pence.

5th. That any person racing, riding or driving at an immoderate rate through the streets of the Town, shall be liable to a fine not exceeding thirty shillings.

6th. That any person driving any description of sleigh within the limits of the Town, without having two or more bells affixed to the harness of the horse drawing same, and shall do injury to any person or property shall be fined in not less than two shillings and sixpence.

7th. That any oxen, horses, sheep, cows, or swine found trespassing on any garden or other property within the Town, the same being enclosed by a lawful fence, shall be held subject to any damage sustained, and if any dispute arise between the proprietor of the garden or other property and the owner of the animal or animals impounded, it shall and may be lawful for the pound-keeper to call upon the Assessor of the Town to assess the damage; and the amount so awarded shall be final and conclusive, and the said assessor shall be entitled to the sum of two shillings and six pence for his trouble, and in default of payment the distress to be sold by public auction, on the pound keeper giving four days notice if the owner lives within the limits of the Town, and then if otherwise, and the overplus, if any, to be paid to the owner after deducting costs and charges.

8th. That any swine found running at large within the limits of the Town shall be liable to be impounded and held subject (when no damage has been sustained) to the payment of two shillings and six pence, besides poundage fees; one half of the fine to go to the person or persons driving them to the pound; and if not released by the owner or owners within twenty four hours, the animal or animals to be advertised giving three days notice (if owner within the limits of the Town) and if no claiment appears and there shall be reason to suppose the animal or animals belong to, or are owned, by persons living out and at a distance from the precincts of the Town, a notice of ten days shall be given and then, if not sooner released, they shall be sold, and the pound keeper is hereby empowered to sell them, at the expiration of ten days, at one o'clock in the afternoon, and after deducting therefrom fees and expenses for keeping the same, the balance, if any, shall be paid to the owner, or in case no claimant appears, into the hands of the treasurer subject to the order of the Board.

9th. That any person convicted of rescuing, or attempting to rescue any swine, cattle, horses or sheep, taken up in conformity with any regulation or order of the Board, shall forfeit and pay a sum, no exceeding twenty shillings for every such offence.

10th. That if any person after the first day of July next shall continue to keep an open house or grocery within the Town where provisions and liquors not distilled are sold to be eaten and drunk therein, or shall presume after the first of July next aforesaid to open a house for such purposes without having obtained a license to do so. He, she or they shall forfeit and pay a sum of one pound.

11th. That the Bar Room door of all public houses, and groceries be closed for the night at 10 o'clock in the evening and shall be kept closed during the whole of the Sabbath day, except for the admittance of travellers, not inhabitants of the town, under penalty not exceeding 30 shillings.

12th. That any person or persons who shall suffer drinking, gaming or fighting or any other disorderly conduct in the house occupied by him, her or them to the disturbance of his, her, or their neighbours shall for each and every such offence forfeit and pay a sum not less than 10 s.

13th. That if any person or persons shall injure or destroy any trees planted for shade or ornament in Town, or shall pull down or deface any sign board or shall inscribe or draw any indecent words, figures or pictures on any building or other public place in the Town, or shall raise or make disturbance in any place or places of public worship, or be found guilty of profane oaths, cursing, execrations, fighting, drunkeness, uncleanliness or other scandalous behavior, or any disturbances by noise or otherwise to the annoyance of the inhabitants of the Town, shall for each and every of the said offences forfeit and pay a sum not exceeding one pound ten shillings, nor less than five shillings at the discretion of the Board.

14th. That if any persons shall after the first day of July next be found selling bread under the following standard, to wit, loaf 4 lb., 1/2 loaf 2 lb., 1/4 loaf 1 lb., they shall for each and every such offence forfeit and pay the sum of 2 s 6d. And further if any person or persons shall knowingly put into any wheaten bread made for sale, any mixture of mead or flour of any other sort of grain than the same shall import to be, or shall adulterate any wheaten bread which shall be made for sale with any mixture or ingredient not allowed to be used in the making of Bread, shall forfeit and pay for each and every of the said offences the sum of 15s.

15th. That any person having deposited or caused to be deposited, or shall hereafter deposit or cause to be deposited, in any street of the town, timber, boards, planks, stones, brick, lime mortar, or other materials for building and who shall refuse, or neglect to remove the same within twenty four hours after having been directed by the street surveyor so to do, shall forfeit and pay a penalty of not less than 5s, for every offence and the further sum of two shillings and six pence for every 24 hours thereafter that the same shall be suffered to remain. Provided that this regulation shall not extend to persons requiring such materials for immediate use and occupying therewith not more than half the width of the street opposite the site of the intended building.

16th. That any person depositing in any street of this Town any firewood, cart, wagon, or other carriage, cask, case, rubbish or filth of any description except with the intention of immediate removal, and who shall neglect forthwith to remove the same upon being directed by any member of the corporation or the Street Surveyor so to do, shall forfeit and pay the sum of 5s. for every such neglect or refusal.

17th. Every chimney or flue in which a fire is commonly made shall from the 1st. of November to the 1st. of April in every year be swept at least once in every 8 weeks and when the same is daily used for Kitchens, and Manufactories, once in every eight weeks throughout the year in the same manner by the Tennant or person authorized and every person neglecting to comply with this regulation shall forfeit and pay on conviction thereof a sum not less than five shillings.

18th. That all Poundkeepers appointed under this Board shall render an account on or before the first Monday in each month to this Board of all penalties forefeited by them and pay over the same to the Treasurer within twenty-four hours thereinafter under the penalty of five shillings.

19th. Any person who shall refuse or neglect to signify to the clerk of the said Corporation, in writing, his dissent to enter upon the service of any office to which he may be appointed by the said Corporation, for the space of three days after receiving notice of such appointment, shall forfeit and pay the sum of not less than 5s. for every such neglect or refusal.

20th. That it shall be the duty of the Assessor to take down every Lot, occupied or not occupied, within the limits of the said town, and the persons residing within the said limits are required to define the Lot on which there is a building

The Ward in which it is situated, the Lot, and what part of it, so that no doubt can be entertained as to the identical Building, House and Lot. Any person neglecting or refusing to give any or all of these particulars on the information or complaint of the Assessor shall be subject and liable to pay a fine of not less than 10s., and in the event of their still refusing, for each subsequent refusal to be subject and liable to pay a further penalty of not less than 20s., and the Assessors are hereby strictly enjoined to carry this order into effect.

21st. That it shall be the duty of the Assessor at the time of the Assessment to take a census of the population within the limits of the town, and all persons are hereby enjoined to make correct returns to the Assessor of each and every resident within his, her or their house, under a penalty of not less than 10s.

22d. No person shall be allowed to exhibit any Wax Figures, Puppet Shows, Rope or Wire Dancing in the Town without first paying 30s. for a license for every such exhibition. And no person or persons shall be allowed to exhibit or expose to view any Caravans of Wild Beasts, or any animals, within said Town, or exhibit Pictures for the purpose of gain, or get any Circus or Theatrical Entertainment for public admission without first taking out a license for every such exhibition and paying for it as follows: Caravans of Wild Beasts, Circuses, and Theatrical Entertainments 50s. each. Exhibition of Pictures and views 20s. for each exhibition.

23d. That all occupiers of Houses within the limits of the Town shall on or before the first of October next provide and keep in repair one ladder to reach the eave of his, her or their dwelling House and one other to reach from the eave to the top of the roof there of to be placed as occasion may require; under a penalty of not less than 2s. 6d. nor more than 30s.

24th. All persons are forbidden fishing with torches or other fire lights within 600 feet of the bridge situated at Mr. Ham's Mill, every person so offending shall be liable in a penalty of not less than 5s.

25th. That all officers of the Board of Police who shall wilfully neglect or refuse to perform the several duties of their respective offices shall be liable, upon due complaint and proof of such refusal or neglect, to pay a fine of not less than five shillings.

26th. Any person who shall disobey the summons or subpoena, of the Board, shall for every such offence forfeit and pay a sum not exceeding 30s. and any person who shall be guilty of obstructing any bailiff, constable, or other officer of Police in the excercise of his or their duty shall forfeit and pay a fine of not exceeding 30s.

Any person or persons who shall be guilty of any disorderly conduct to the Board while sitting shall be subject to fine and imprisonment at the discretion of the Board.

28th. That three Members of the Board shall constitute a quorum and may appoint a chairman and proceed with business in the absence of the President.

EBENEZER PERRY, President of Police.

Cobourg, 28th June, 1837.

APPENDIX

Officers appointed by the Board of Police for the Town of Cobourg with a table of their respective fees.

CLERK AND ASSESSOR   James Lambert
COLLECTOR, STREET SURVEYOR and BAILIFF   William Grigg
CONSTABLES   James Tremble, George Birney, Richard Brown, George Edgecomb
POUNDKEEPERS   S.P. Hart, J.B.F. Cotter
TREASURER   Robert Henry, Esq. Commercial Bank

CLERK's FEES

Information	2s. 6d.
Warrant	2s. 6d.
Summons	0s. 6d.
Subpoena	0s. 6d.
Conviction	2s. 6d.
Execution	2s. 0d.

CONSTABLES FEES

Service of Warrant	5.s 0d.
Service of Summons	1s. 4d.
Service of Subpoena	1s. 4d.
Service of Execution	2s. 0d.
Service of Advertising	1s. 6d.
Selling and making return	2s. 6d.
Removing property to be charged extra.	

POUNDKEEPER's FEES

Impounding Horses, Oxen & Cows	9d.
Feeding per diem	9d.
Impounding sheep or pigs	6d.
Feeding per Diem	6d.
Impounding young cattle under two years old	5d.
Feeding per diem Do. Do.	6d.

Rates of Feeding

That every Horse, Ox, or Cow shall be allowed 16 lb. of Hay, young Cattle 10 lb. Sheep 2½ lb. and pigs one quart of Peas per diem.

-- From the Cobourg Star, July 12, 1837

The New Town

In the raising of Cobourg from a Police Village to an incorporated town, administered by a five member Board of Police, a number of changes took place. Up to and including the 30th of June, 1837, Cobourg was still part of Hamilton Township. The Township officers performed for the village streets. The District Magistrates meeting in Quarter Sessions were still in authority, and the fire department and fire prevention regulations were under their oversight. The Act of Incorporation did NOT specify a date as to when the change – over was to become effective. This date naming was left to the President and Board of Police. This elected body drafted a set of rules and regulations, appointed their officers, set fees and applied the date of JULY 1st, 1837, for the changeover to take place. On July 1st, 1837, the Town of Cobourg was born.

What does this mean? The town now had defined boundaries, the area withing which became separated from the jurisdiction of Hamilton Township. The area included the Police Village of Amherst and the White's Mills – Hull's Corners hamlet, located on Division Street North. Cobourg became the District Town, with the Gaol and Court House inside its boundaries. The President and Board of Police had acquired both administrative and judicial powers, applied within the boundaries of the Corporation. The District Magistrates meeting in Quarter Sessions no longer ruled in Cobourg. Likewise the Hamilton Township Annual Town Meeting. The Fire Department came under the town administration. The President and Board of Police were empowered to hold court for infractions of their By-Laws, and levy fines. The Town was an entirely new and separate municipality, with a governing body legalized to promote and to carry out local improvements, apply taxes, borrow money, and in general look after the well being of the town.

The Public Market

The subject of a market place had been a contentious local issue for nearly six years. Now that a President and Board of Police was in power, action towards obtaining land for a public market was taken. The following is recorded:

"NOTICE is hereby given, that proposals containing offers of land for a market site within the Town of Cobourg, with prices and terms of payment, will be received by the Board of Police until the 15th day of August, next.

(Signed)E. PERRY, President.
JAMES LAMBERT, Clerk".

Board of Police,
July 17, 1837.

"Standing Order – The Board of Police meet at their Clerk's office every Monday at 8 o'clock in the morning."

-- The Cobourg Star, July 19, 1837.

The above was followed up with a statement later by the President of the Board:
"Notice is hereby given, that the President and Board of Police have chosen as the intended site for the Market Place in the Town of Cobourg, the lot of land on which Mr. Freeman S. Clench at present resides, containing nearly one acre and a quarter, having a front of about 147 feet on the south side of King Street.

EBENEZER PERRY, President of Police".

"Board of Police, Cobourg
September 4, 1837."

-- The Cobourg Star, September 6, 1837.

About this time, Mr. Abraham Crouter purchased some sixty acres of Cobourg in the vicinity of University Avenue, west of Spring Street. He was promoting sub-divisions and selling town lots. It may have been in this area that he made an offer to the town of an acre of land for a market. His public statement is of interest:

" TO THE FREE AND INDEPENDENT ELECTORS OF THE TOWN OF COBOURG"

"Since my removal to this place, I have felt a deep interest for its improvement; and to save the people from taxation and enable myself to take a further stand in its improvement, I have offered one acre of land, without price, for a market; but the Board of Police have chosen another place, at 1,000 Pounds, and will wish me to help pay for it, and rather than do it, I will give with the acre security for the payment; and if the inhabitants of the Town of Cobourg refuse this offer, I shall keep the acre and fifty Pounds and do something else with(it).

"I remain, your sincere friend, and well-wisher,
A. CROUTER."

"Cobourg September 12, 1837."

-- The Cobourg Star, September 13, 1837.

The site chosen for a Public Market, to the west of Second Street was not acceptable to some people. The President and Board of Police called a public meeting to finalize the issue. The meeting notice is given here:

"NOTICE - A protest signed by twelve voters in town, against the site chosen for a market by the Board of Police, having been laid before the said Board."
"Notice is hereby given that a general meeting of the inhabitants, voters in the town, will be held in the Common School House, on Tuesday the 3rd of October next, at 12 o'clock noon, for the purpose of confirming or rejecting said Market site within the Town.

E. PERRY, President.
JAMES LAMBERT, Clerk.

"Board of Police, Cobourg, September 27, 1837."

-- The Cobourg Star, September 27, 1837.

At the public meeting, the site chosen by the Board of Police was confirmed.

Purchase of properties proceeded and Mr. F.S. Clench acted as agent for the town. Between Second and Third Streets, there were at least three buildings facing on King Street. The westerly one remained in private ownership. The next was Mr. Clench's residence. The third one may have been a place of business, or a residence. The group of properties were deeded to the town and Registered on May 14, 1838, consisting of lots Numbers five and six, seven and the east half of Lot Number nine, all in Block B.

Three newspaper articles, given below, are of interest. An Editorial – We heartily congratulate the people of Cobourg that there really is at length some probability of their possessing the advantage of a market. At the meeting yesterday, called to ascertain the sense of the inhabitants generally upon the site chosen by the Board of Police, namely the property offered by Mr. F.S. Clench, situated on the south side of King Street, with the buildings thereon, owned and occupied by him--it was most unanimously resolved to confirm the same, and the purchase is to be effected accordingly. We may hope soon to see therefore provisions in Cobourg as reasonable in price as elsewhere.

-- The Cobourg Star, October 4, 1837.

An Editorial – IMPROVEMENTS IN COBOURG

We feel called upon to notice with hearty commendation the activity and zeal displayed by our new Board of Police; under whose efficient management the advantages of the Act of Incorporation for the Town of Cobourg are in course of steady development. In addition to the very judicious and valuable selection of a market site, before noticed, we have now to applaud the improvement, of scarcely inferior importance to our comfort, which is at present in progress, namely the construction of side-walks in the principle streets. They are to be of wood, similar to those so much approved of in Toronto, and will, in the first instance, we understand, extend east and west, from the English to the Scotch Church, a distance a little short of a mile; and north and south from the Methodist Chapel to the wharf.

-- The Cobourg Star, October 18, 1837.

"WANTED TO BORROW – By the President and Board of Police of the Town of Cobourg, for not less than one, or more than five years, the sum of 500 Pounds in sums of not less than 50 Pounds, on the security of the town. Interest six percent.

EBENEZER PERRY, President, Board of Police."

"Board of Police, Cobourg, November 27, 1837."

-- The Cobourg Star, November 29, 1837.

Board of Trade in Cobourg

A meeting of the merchants and others interested in the trade of Cobourg was

First Land Purchase
by the
Town of Cobourg 1838

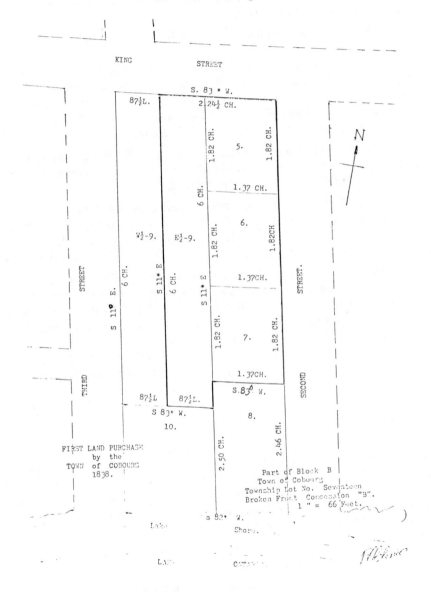

held at the Albion Hotel on Saturday, the 2nd instant, to take into consideration the expediency of establishing a Board of Trade.

The Hon. Walter Boswell was called to the chair, and Kenneth Mackenzie was appointed Secretary, when it was:

Moved by E. Perry, Esq., and seconded by B. Throop, Esq.,

1st. That in order to afford more facilities for regulating various matters connected with the local, as well as the general interests of trade, this meeting deems it highly expedient that the trading portion of the community of this Town should establish a Board of Trade, to be guided by such rules and regulations as may hereinafter be adopted.

Moved by W.W. Boswell, Esq., and seconded by W. Graveley, Esq.,

2nd. That this meeting do now form itself into a Board of Trade; and be called "THE COBOURG BOARD OF TRADE."

Moved by J.V. Boswell, Esq., and seconded by Mr. John McCarty,

3rd. That the following gentlemen, viz – E. PERRY, G. HAM, W.S. CONGER, B. THROOP, J.C. BOSWELL, and C. MORGAN, Esqs., be appointed to draw up rules and regulations for the guidance of the Board of Trade.

Moved by George Ham, Esq., and seconded by W.E. Conger, esq.

4th. That a meeting of the Board take place at the Albion Hotel, on Monday evening, the 11th instant, at half past seven o'clock to adopt the rules and regulations for the guidance of the Board, and to elect a Committee of Management for the current year.

W. BOSWELL, Chairman.
K. MACKENZIE, secretary.

-- The Cobourg Star, September 6, 1837.

Queen Victoria

In relating the story of the birth of the Town of Cobourg, we have passed by other interesting events. On June 20th, 1837, His Majesty, King William the Fourth had passed away. On June 21st, Queen Victoria became the Monarch of the Realm, only ten days before Cobourg became a town. The news of these two events did not reach Cobourg until the 2nd of August.

The Rebellion

Late in November of 1837, rebellion broke out in Lower Canada. The regular soldiers were sent to that province, leaving only militia units in Upper Canada. Events took a serious turn, and men were needed for any emergency that may arise. The following notice appeared in the Cobourg Star of November 29th, 1837:

"To the Young Men of Cobourg."

"It is proposed, with permission of the executive, to form a Volunteer Rifle Company in Cobourg, to be attached to the First Regiment of Northumberland Militia, with the usual privileges and conditions. All persons in the town and neighbourhood, whose loyalty at the present moment of threatened revolution in the sister province, may prompt them to join such company, with a desire for immediate active service, can please leave their names at this office." (The editor, Mr. R.D. CHATTERTON was active in the Militia.)

The Cobourg Rifles were organized under Captain Edward Warren, a Cobourg resident and a veteran of the 66th Regiment. The following is the list of names, mostly young men of Cobourg, that composed this unit.

The Cobourg Rifles.
Captain Warren, late of the 66th Regiment.
Lieutenants - Chatterton, McDonald, late of the 59th, and H. Covert ·
Qr. Master Ser'gt - H.E. Nichols
Sergents - G.M. Goodeve and H.H. Meredith.
Corporals - Saunders and R. Armour.
Privates:

Charles Perry	C.G. Buller	C.S. Finlayson	George Pierce
Rowe Buck	Wm. Graveley	W.W. Hammond	Marsh
J. McGarvey	R.H. Throop	R.D. Rogers	Jonathan E.
F.H. Burton	Wm. Butler	C.J. Owston	Tremain
H.W. Jones	Charles Butler	John Laurie	Henry Falkner
W.F. Harper	Wm. Boswell	Henry Blackstone	A.G. Allan
Wm. Bancks	James Mewburn Jr.	Angus Crawford	F.P. Covert
			— Brady
			Henry J. Ruttan

"Of the officers, Warren and McDonald had served in the line. Owing to their exertions, the Cobourg Rifles were better organized than any other volunteer corps on the Frontier."

- The Adventures of the Cobourg Rifles

Suddenly, without warning, the Yonge Street uprising under William Lyon MacKenzie broke out. The Lieutenant Governor called out the Militia. The order was received in Cobourg on Tuesday night, December 5th. The various Colonels were ordered to mobilize their regiments. The flank companies were to advance on Toronto, the others were to hold themselves in readiness to march on an hour's notice.

Early Thursday morning, December 7th, the several volunteer companies began to assemble. The time had come to march. It was only a few days earlier that the Cobourg Rifles were recruited. This company formed the advance for the march to Toronto. They were followed by Captain Clark and Captain Calcutt's companies. Captain Conger, with his men, brought up the rear. The volunteer cavalry, under the command of Captain Rogers, left Cobourg for Toronto on the Friday. In all, some 2,000 men from the Newcastle District answered the call to duty.

It was a difficult march to Toronto and occupied three days. The Cobourg Rifles had no route march experience, and they had to contend with muddy, clay roads under winter conditions. When they reached Toronto, the Yonge Street affair had been overcome, the rebels had fled to the Niagara River and took possession of Navy Island, above the falls.

Volunteers were called for at Toronto to defend the Niagara Frontier, and the Cobourg Rifles responded. They were despatched to Chippawa.

The steamer "Caroline" was employed by the Rebels to communicate between Navy Island and the American shore. A Canadian raiding party crossed the river after dark, located the steamer on the American side, boarded the boat, subdued the crew on board, then cut the boat loose from its moorings, set it on fire, and left the boat to let it drift downstream. It disappeared over Niagara Falls as a flaming torch. The raiding party returned safely to the Candian shore in their small boats. Captain Warren and perhaps others in the Cobourg Rifles took part in the raid on the "Caroline". The incident became an international affair. By late January of 1838, the rebels were dispersed. Navy Island was abandoned after heavy shelling, and the Niagara Frontier became quiet. The men from Cobourg returned home.

The Rebellion left much uncertainty in its wake. Political affairs were in a disordered state, and the fears of rebel raiding parties from the United States added to the insecurity. The economy of the province went into a decline. In general, conditions were not encouraging and local developments were held back pending better times.

The first Monday in June was election time again for Cobourg. This time William Weller, George Ham, E. Perry, Asa Burnham and W.S. Conger were the Board of Police for the ensuing year. The general account of the town for its first year of operation is given here. A few of the items listed were difficult to decipher.

GENERAL ACCOUNT of the TOWN OF COBOURG, May 26, 1838
DR.
1837

		£.	s.	d.
July 4,	To A. Rubidge, Printing and Adverstising account, Per Receipt.	2	10	0
Aug. 19,	To J. Davis, fixing and clearing well	0	15	0
Aug. 20,	J. McCarty and Co., 114 feet of lumber	0	4	0
Aug. 21,	To A. Jeffrey, Hinges, nails Etc for well cover . . .	0	5	3
Sept. 4.	To Foster Sprague, for repairs on Fire Engine . . .	0	13	0
Sept. 4,	To H. Dumble, Stone to Bridge	0	5	6
Sept. 4,	To J. Trimble, Repairing "do"	0	16	0

Sept. 4,	To Norton & Musser, Office Furniture	2	0	0
Sept. 4,	To Blacksmith work to well	0	2	6
Sept. 27,	To William Grigg, 2 cedar logs and 4 planks....	0	4	0
Oct. 13,	To J. Whitaker, drawing gravel to streets	0	6	8
Oct. 28,	To Note in Commercial Bank.......(25 Pounds)	25	0	0
Nov. 3,	M. Purser, fixing fire hooks...................	0	7	6
Nov. 27,	To Note in Commercial Bank	20	0	0
1838				
Jan. 20,	To Starling and Keeler, for making drains	9	13	6
Jan. 20,	To J. Fisher, for logs to "do"..................	0	5	0
Mar. 2,	To W.S. Conger, per Z. Sisson, towards side walks	4	0	10
Mar. 3,	To A. Rubidge, Printing and advertising account	4	15	11
March 14,	To J. Bain, Painting Constable's Batons, etc	1	2	6
Mar. 14,	To T.L. ? For Minute Book	1	10	0
Mar. 14,	To Richard Solomon Black Smith Work	0	8	3
Mar. 28,	To F.S. Clench, Taxes returned on account	2	6	0
April 3,	To F.S. Clench, First instalment on Market Site .	250	0	0
May 1st,	To F.S. Clench, Rent of R. West, assumed	12	16	8
May 1st,	To F.S. Clench, Rent of Dyer, assumed	0	15	0
May 7,	To Paid to Police Ledger.....................	2	16	0
May 7,	To William Grigg Account, for services as Street Surveyor	9	18	0
May 7,	To Wm. Grigg, Collectors fees off £211 5s 2d ...	10	11	3
May 7,	To Edward Hales, Services as Fire Inspector.....	2	9	6
May 7,	To Wm. Grigg, Registering Deed of Market Site .	1	0	0
May 7,	To W.S. Conger, per Account of sidewalks	59	0	0
May 7,	To ? ?, per Account of sidewalks	4	2	0
May 7,	To Police for Salary	17	10	0
May 12,	To ? ? For repairing Bridge...................	2	9	0
May	To Postage	0	3	8
May ?,	To ? (poor copy) ? Returning	5	4	6
May	To ? ? ? Collectors fees off ?	2	13	0
May	To ? ? Overseeing improvements to Market Site ..	3	11	0
May ?,	To James Lambert, Account of Clerk's Fees in ? no connection..............................	1	18	9
May	To F. Sprague Account, repairs to fire engine	1	18	9
May	To account work done on streets	38	6	0
May	To For work done on Market site for taxes......	7	7	10½
May ?,	Amount of Money in Mr. Grigg's Hands	2	14	2½
May	To Amount of discounts paid to Commercial Bank on a note of 102 Pounds, 10s and of 60			

	pound note given to renew said note by W.S. Conger	2	9	10
May	Amount in Treasurer's hands	1	1	7½
		518	2	3½

May 26,	To Balance due W.S. Conger on Notes	160	0	0
May 26,	To "do" "do" "do" On Account	33	1	10½
May 26,	To Balance due F.S. Clench on Account	14	12	4½
May 26,	To Balance due John McCarty on account	2	2	10½
May 26,	To Balance due R.D. Chatterton on Account	2	7	1
May 26,	To Balance due Donald Bethune on account	5	0	0
		217	4	2

May 26,	To Balance due by the Town of Cobourg	213	8	4½

Cr.
1837

July 1st,	By License to Circus and Menagerie	5	0	0
October 28,	By Proceeds of Note, 25 Pounds in Com. Bank	24	12	4
Novemb. 27,	By Proceeds of Note, 20 Pounds in Com. Bank	19	14	0
March 12,	By Amount of taxes, Etc collected by W. Grigg, including subscriptions to sidewalks	211	5	2
March 12,	By Amount of fines collected by the Board	3	7	3
March 12,	By Amount of Pound-Keeper's returns	3	17	7
March 12,	By Amount of Statute Labour money for 1837	6	2	2
March 12,	By Amount of J. McCarty's taxes remitted on account	4	2	0
May 1st,	By Amount of house-rent of R. West, assumed by F.S.Clench	12	16	8
May 1st	By Amount of House-rent of Dyer, assumed by F.S. Clench	0	15	0
May 22,	By Amount of taxes collected by J. Trimbles	53	12	6
May 26,	By Amount of taxes collected by J. Trimbles	5	9	9
May 26,	By Amount of work done on the Market-Site for taxes	7	7	10½
May 26,	By Balance — W.S. Conger's Note given to G.S. Boulton for Corporation .... 100 Pounds.			
May 26,	And W.S. Conger's Note given to the COMMERCIAL BANK for Corporation........ 60 Pounds.			
		160	0	0
		518	2	3½

1837
May 26, By Amount in Mr. Grigg's hands 2 14 2½
May 26, By Amount in Treasurer's hands.   1   1 7½
May 26, Balance Due by the Corporation. 213   8 4½

                                                          217   4 2½

                                              EBENEZER PERRY,
                                           President Board of Police
Cobourg May 26, 1838   — — The Cobourg Star, May 30, 1838

No report in the Cobourg Star re the 1838 Municipal elections.

AT A MEETING — of the Board of Police for the Town of Cobourg, on the
18th Day of June, 1838, the following appointments were made, viz: —
  CLERK and ASSESSOR — — — Kenneth Mackenzie,
  Collector, Street Surveyor and Bailiff — — James Tremble.
  Constables — J.B.F. Cotter, Thomas Salisbury.
  Pound Keepers, — J.B.F. Cotter; George Hart.
  TREASURER, Robert Henry, Esq. Commercial Bank.
RESOLVED: — That the Board meet in the Town Hall, at eight o'clock on
Monday morning, in each week, for the transaction of business.
                              GEORGE HAM, President of Police.
Cobourg, 18th June, 1838   — — — The Cobourg Star, June 20, 1838.

It appears that one of the buildings purchased by the town, was converted in
total or in part for use as a town hall. The remainder of the buildings were rented to private individuals, and occupied the site of to-day's Victoria Hall in part.

Coronation of Queen Victoria

Thursday June 28th, 1838, was set aside for the Coronation of Queen Victoria.
Cobourg joined in with many other places in celebrating this event. The Cobourg
Star tells us:
  "Thursday last being the day named for the Coronation of our most gracious Queen, the loyal inhabitants of Cobourg, resolved not to be behind-
  hand with their brethren of Toronto, Kingston and elsewhere, did all honor
  to the happy event by a very general and brilliant illumination, accompanied by a display of fireworks, firing of guns, bonfires, etc., altogether making up a very respectable celebration."

Militia Activated

For most of the year of 1838, and on into 1839, the militia of the Province was maintained to full strength, with training days and at other times acting on guard duty. There was the ever present fear of raiding parties making sorties into upper Canada from the United States.

The muster of Militia in Cobourg for general training on Monday the 4th of June, 1838, was the largest yet experienced. One month later, three local companies under Captains Conger, Calcutt and Chatterton, some 130 men, fully armed and equipped, were dispatched to Whitby in anticipation of an outbreak of trouble. After four days, they were returned to Cobourg by boat.

By November, the government sponsored extensive military preparation. There was a tense feeling of invasion throughout the province. The Cobourg Colonels of Militia were directed to call out two companies of 100 men each from their respective regiments, for six months of active guard duty in other places. Another group, under Lieut-Col. Bethune was stationed in Cobourg for six months. They were disbanded at the end of the following April.

The steamboat "COBOURG" was armed and placed on patrol duty in November, as a precaution against a shore landing of rebels. This boat was assigned to cover the shoreline of the Newcastle District from Presqu'ile to Windsor Bay.

In the brief form presented here, these notes may give the reader an insight to the steps taken by the authorities to protect the province through the years following the outbreak of rebellion.

Cobourg Churches

Earlier in this history, reference was made to the Methodists, the Presbyterians, and the Church of England. Many of the newcomers to Upper Canada sought to establish in their new community the kind of church to which they had been accustomed in their homeland. The immigrants came from a variety of religious backgrounds, and Cobourg newcomers were of no exception. "Where two or three are gathered to-gether" a church service of worship was held in a home or some available space.

By the year 1835, a few families of Congregational Church backgound were living in Cobourg. The reverend William Hayden, and his large family arrived in Cobourg from Frodingham, Yorkshire in 1835. He was the missionary type of minister, and came to Canada under the authority of the Colonial Missionary Society of the Congregational Union of England and Wales. He organized a small group of worshippers into a church. A Chapel was erected and opened in 1836 on King Street, on a piece of property now occuped by C.D.C.I. West. The Chapel, of frame construction, provided accomodation for 200 people. Mr. Hayden did not limit his activities to Cobourg, but made the whole Newcastle District his parish. He made many arduous journeys on horseback to remote settlers, ministering to their religious needs. Ten years after his arrival, Hayden and his family moved to Cold Springs, where he established a second church and lived out the rest of his life. Mrs. Hayden was a strong helpmate to her husband. In addition to the caring of the family, she organized and supervised the first Sunday School to be held in Cobourg in the year of their arrival in 1835.

The Bible Christian movement, an offshoot of the Methodist denomination, had its beginnings in the Duchy of Cornwall, England. By 1835 a number of families of Cornish origin had come to Cobourg and to the Newcastle District. It was about this time a group of this denomination met for worship in a building on Orange Street. As their numbers increased, a church was organized. In later years a fine brick church was erected and occupied by the Bible Christians at the north-west corner of James and Bond Streets.

It is reported the Roman Catholic folk, though few in number, became active about the year 1837, and started a fund for the erection of a church building. By 1839, under the leadership of Father Kernan, their plans were realized by the erection of a frame building located on the east side of William Street at a spot presently occupied by the General Foods Research building. This church was dedicated with the name of St. Polycarp, and the parish extended into the countryside. Sheriff Henry Ruttan donated the land and Mr. William Solomon donated the timber for the building. The congregation prospered and in a few short years outgrew the accomodation of the frame building.

In those early years of growth for the young village, the physical expansion was paralleled with growth and development of religious denominations. The worship of God was by no means neglected.

A Strange Twist

The Town of Cobourg was incorporated in the year 1837. For the first two years after its formation, Mr. George Ham, the owner of the a large property and industries in the west end of the town, had been elected twice and held a seat on the Board of Police. He even served as President of Police in 1838. The severe controversy over organizing a town that went on since 1832, just would not go away. The Cobourg Star of March 27, 1839, reported the following about petitions to the central government:

"Legislative Council, Monday March 18, 1839"

"Of Mr. George Ham and two hundred and six others, of the Town of Cobourg, praying that the Act incorporating the said Town be repealed."

Some events take on a strange twist at times.

Town Affairs

We report here several transcripts taken from the Cobourg Star newspaper issues of 1839, dealing with town affairs which are of interest.

"ELECTION" — "The election of the Board of Police took place on the 3rd instant, when Messers. CONGER, WELLER, D'ARCY E. BOULTON, LAWDER and CROUTER were chosen for the Board for the ensuing year;

the three first without opposition, the other two by a majority of five, on a poll with George Ham, Esquire. At a subsequent meeting of the Board, Wilson S. Conger was appointed President, and Mr. Hargraft, Clerk."

— — The Cobourg Star, June 11, 1839.

"TO CONTRACTORS" — "Notice is hereby given that sealed tenders will be received at this office until Monday the 24th, instant, at 9 o'clock A.M. from persons willing to contract for the erection of a "Market House" in the Town of Cobourg.

"Plans and Specifications may be seen at the office of W.S. Conger, Esq. W.S. CONGER, President, Board of Police.

"Police Office, Cobourg, June 11, 1839."

— — The Cobourg Star, June 19, 1839.

"WANTED" — — "Persons willing to contract for the furnishing materials and laying down a planked "Side-walk' from the corner of Spring and King Streets to the Scotch Church.

"By Order"

W.S. Conger, President, Board of Police."

"Police Office, Cobourg, June 11, 1839."

— — The Cobourg Star, June 19, 1839.

"THE COBOURG MARKET BUILDING" —

"The new market building for this town, built under direction of the Board of Police, was opened to the public on Monday last, and has since been an object of considerable attraction. The advantages are manifest, and we sincerely congratulate the inhabitants of Cobourg upon the establishment of an institution so requisite for their comfort, and which will so certainly advance the prosperity of their town. The building is exceedingly neat and commodious without being expensive, and reflects great credit on the taste and judgment of the Board. Mr. Donald McDonald has been appointed Market Clerk."

— — The Cobourg Star, October 30, 1839.

"RULES and REGULATIONS for the PUBLIC MARKET of the TOWN OF COBOURG."

Passed 22nd of October, 1839.

"Be it enacted by the President and Board of Police of the Town of Cobourg."

"That the Public Market House now erected, and the Market Place adjoining, and established in the Town of Cobourg, shall be the Market House and Market Place thereof; and all butchers and other persons using and frequenting the same, shall be subject to the Rules and Regulations following, from and after the 28th of October, 1839."

(Twenty rules follow.)

"By Order"

"W.S. Conger, President."

— — The Cobourg Star, October 30, 1839.

Market House Costs.

We give here the price paid by the Town of Cobourg for its new Market Building, as reported in the General Accounts of May 1839 to May 20th, 1840.

Sept. 10, 1839 Cash paid F. Burnet, work for Market Building . 56 5 0

Feb. 13, 1840 Paid to F. Burnet, per account 14 15 4

April 27,
1840   Paid F. Burnet, pd. in full for Market House . . . 56 5 0

TOTAL 127 5 4

May 19, 1840 Pd. Insuring Market House 0 9 10

D. E. Boulton, Member, Board of Police.
David Brodie, Clerk, Board of Police.
— — The Cobourg Star, May 26, 1840.

Shin-Plasters

By late 1839, the economy in general was improving. The following is a bit of good news in the direction of better times, as reported in the Cobourg Star:

"A meeting of Merchants was held in Cobourg last evening, pursuant to notice at which was adopted the following wholesome resolution:

"IT WAS RESOLVED, that in consequence of the Banks of Upper Canada having resumed specie payments, this meeting deem it advisable to decline taking shin-plasters after the 1st of december next."

"DONALD McDONALD, Secretary.   CHARLES H. MORGAN, Chairman."

— — The Cobourg Star, November 20, 1839.

The Marriage of Queen Victoria

The formal announcement of Queen Victoria's marriage, made by the Privy Council, was reported in the Cobourg Star of March 11th, 1840. The actual marriage to His Royal Highness, Prince Albert of Saxe-Coburg-Gothe took place on the 10th of February, at noon, at the Chapel Royal St. Jame's.

The Cobourg Star newspaper featured this event with a long, detailed story in the March 18th issue. The Town of Cobourg laid on plans to have a celebration in honor of the marriage, and the Board of Police issued the following instructions:

"ILLUMINATION" — "The President and Board of Police for the Town of Cobourg, having fixed upon Thursday evening, the 2nd Instant, for a general illumination in honour of the Queen's Marriage, request all classes of Her Majesty's loyal and dutiful subjects to join them in the celebration of this joyful event."

"W.S. Conger, President, Board of Police."

"Town Hall, Cobourg,
1st. April, 1840."

"P.S. — To commence at 8 o'clock in the evening and continue until 11 o'clock."

"GOD SAVE THE QUEEN".

— — The Cobourg Star, April 1st, 1840.

The Stage Coach King Advertises

TELEGRAPH LINE — Toronto and Hamilton, by the Lake Road three times a week each way. SIX HORSE COACHES, will leave the general stage office, Toronto, at 8 o'clock every Sunday, Tuesday and Thursday morning for Hamilton; and Burley's Hotel, Hamilton for Toronto every Monday, Wednesday and Friday morning at the same hour.

The proprietor having gone to great expense in fitting out this line with new coaches of a superior description, flatters himself, that for comfort, speed and regularity, it will be surpassed by none on the continent of North America.

A Mail stage by Dundas Street, will leave Toronto for Hamilton as usual every day at 12 o'clock, noon (Sunday's excepted) and Hamilton for Toronto, every evening at 10 o'clock (Sundays excepted).

WILLIAM WELLER, Proprietor

THE TORONTO & KINGSTON MAIL STAGE will leave Toronto for Kingston, every Sunday morning at 9 o'clock, and every Monday, Tuesday, Wednesday, and Friday at 5 o'clock p.m. — and Kingston, every morning (Sundays excepted) at 9 o'clock — passing through Scarborough, Pickering, Whitby, Darlington, Clarke, Port Hope, Cobourg, Grafton, Colborne, Brighton, Port Trent, Belleville, Shannonville, Napanee, and Bath — going through in forty-six hours.

The above lines of stages are in connection with those westward, to Queenston and to London, Sandwich and Detroit; Also the stages at Kingston for Montreal and Quebec, and Watertown, Utica, Albany, and New York.

EXTRAS and EXPRESSES furnished at all times, at Toronto, Cobourg, Belleville and Kingston on reasonable terms.

Seats taken at the General Stage Office, Toronto and Kingston. Thirty pounds of baggage allowed to each passenger. All extra 200 pounds equal to a passenger's fare. All baggage at risk of owner.

PROPRIETORS — W. Weller, Toronto and River Trent.

R. Munroe, River Trent and Kingston

Cobourg, 14th December, 1839

— The Cobourg Star, January 1st, 1840.

X/THE LARGER SPHERE OF COMMUNITY

With reference to the country and the larger sphere of things, and as a result of the 1837 Rebellion, the British Government sent JOHN GEORGE LAMB-TON, the First Earl of Durham, known as Lord Durham, as Governor General of the five provinces in 1838. He had orders to investigage, report, and make recommendations on the conditions in the Canadas. The famous Durham Report and the political changes that followed are well recorded in histories. The Act of Union was passed in the year of 1840, creating the Province of Canada, which became effective in early 1841.

On the local scene, a writer addressed an interesting letter to the Cobourg Star. It is a thoughtful epistle, reflecting on the times, and we wish to place it before our readers.

To the Editor of the Cobourg Star.
My Dear Sir:

A new leaf in the history of Canada has been turned, and although the previous pages are stained with many faults, yet do they contain many bright and glorious passages. Cultivation is extending over the place of the trackless forest, a hardy, loyal population are converting the lands into gardens of abundance, our rivers and lakes are crowded with boats and their shores studded with rising villages, while the spires of the country churches are beginning to lift their heads in every township. The inhabitants of Upper Canada can look back with pride on their past history; amid trials and difficulties they have adhered steadily to the glorious cause of Monarchy, and when in 1812 the whole available force of the United States was brought against them, they deserted not a single spot, and while their opposers equalled the numbers ten times told, their arms in a righteous cause were ever victorious; and should circumstances again call them forth, the same issue would attend the contest. Henceforth it will be a name of the past, but one, around which many fond recollections will linger, till the present generation shall have passed away, and the silence of the tomb envelop those who fought her battles on the field and in the senate.

In her towns how many wanderers have found a peaceful home. How many from poverty have achieved independence, and how many have learned to esteem and bless that glorious constitution under which we live. It is useless now to question the policy of the union. It were worse than idle to bode evil constantly, and I for one, an humble individual, should deem myself culpable, if through the columns of your journal, I continued to agitate questions over which I can have no control, and with this letter I retire from politics.

During a long connection with the public press, I have ever maintained (what in my opinion were) conservative principles, and I must confess I cannot understand the conduct, the glaring inconsistancy of some who call themselves conservatives; by whom politics and principles seem to be regarded as pivots, on which they can most conveniently turn to worship the rising sun; and, only retire, when I find that my humble but honest endeavours can no longer be of avail to stem the torrent of disunion. Those who come forward as political writers must be prepared to make great sacrifices, and I assure you my career has not been and exception; when I look at this noble District, its natural advantages, with fertile soil not surpassed in the Province, with the means of water communication quite unequalled, with the population rapidly increasing, brave, independent, and attached to the Mother Country, I think that we should be best employed in advocating the cause of public improvement. For this sole noble object, the late event gives an opportunity not to be neglected, and we would act wisely in leaving the troubled waters of political strife and enter into the quiet stream of domestic utility.

. . .We got the seat of government within the limits of Upper Canada (Kingston). We have obtained the English language, but above and before all this, a cloud is gathering around us. . . We should do all in our power to cement the public mind in one bond, and while we differ with the Government on certain questions, loudly to proclaim that we are prepared to uphold its dignity and assert its rights. If we wish for a continuance of our connections with the Mother Country, this is necessary. If we wish to bring peace and happiness among us, this is necessary. I have finished. I retire from politics, my best talents, humble though they are, shall be dedicated to the benefits of this District, and to the bringing forward of its resources.

Yours truly,
ERINENSIS.
— — The Cobourg Star, February 17, 1841.

The New District Council

In June of 1841, the Union Parliament of Canada assembled for the first time in Kingston. On August 27th, an Act was passed to provide for better internal government in Canada West, by establishing provisions for the formation of local or municipal authorities, especially in the Districts.

This Act introduces a new form of District Council, consisting of one or two Councillors elected at the Annual Meeting of each township. The Warden to be appointed by the Governor. The Act gives all the details for the setting up and operation of the new District Council. Self-government and self-taxation are introduced. The Act provides for the transfer of certain powers from the District Magistrates to the District Council.

In late December, it was announced that Captain Walter Boswell had received the appointment of Warden for the new Newcastle District Council.

The Cobourg Star gives us the story about the first District Council meeting:

"The first meeting of the District Council, for the District of Newcastle was held at the Court Room of the Court House, on the 8th. inst. The assemblage of Councillors did not embrace all the Councillors, the present lamentable state of the roads no doubt obstructed the absentees.

"The proceedings opened with the ceremony of reading the Act of the Legislature, which constituted the Council, and the Patent appointing the Warden.

"A short address from the Warden, the Hon. Walter Boswell, declared the Council was duly authorized to proceed in its deliberations, and recommending a careful consideration of all questions of taxation, and to avoid as much as possible, making the taxation burdensome on the people, as is consistant with the improvements essential to the convenience of the public.

"In consequence of the absence of several members of the Council, it was moved by H.S. Reid, Esq., that the nomination of the District Council Officers should be postponed till Wednesday the 9th instant.

"A committee was named by Mr. Weller and adopted, for considering the rules and by-Laws which were submitted to the Council by the Warden.

"On motion of Mr. Weller, all books and papers, refering to measures now falling within the jurisdiction of the District Council were handed over to the acting Clerk of the Council, by Thomas Ward, Esq., Clerk of the Peace.
The Council adjourned its sitting, to 10 o'clock Wednesday morning."
— — The Cobourg Star, February 9th, 1842.

District Divided

Another important change took place in November of 1841. The Newcastle District was divided and the Northern part became the new District of Colborne, centred at Peterborough.

A Cobourg merchant, Mr. Wilson S. Conger received the appointment of Sheriff for the newly formed Colborne District. Mr. Conger had been a very active citizen over the years and he took a leading part in the various Cobourg developments. His resignation from the Board of Police is of interest:
"To the Electors of the East Ward of the Town of Cobourg: —
Gentlemen: — — Having been appointed to an official situation in the new Dis-

trict of Colborne, which must necessarily cause my immediate removal from among you, I deem it my duty to resign this trust I have so long held of representing you in your Municipal Councils, and return you my sincere tkanks for this oft repeated mark of your confidence and respect. Believe me, gentlemen, that it is with no ordinary satisfaction that I look back upon the steady growth and prosperity of the flourishing and happy town, rendered doubly dear to me by all the ties of interest and social happiness. It was here I commenced the world, and I assure you that promising and delightful place of my destination, yet I can never forget the many kindnesses I have received at the hands of the inhabitants of Cobourg, in whose future prosperity I shall always feel the most lively interest."

"I am, gentlemen,
Your most obedient and humble servant.
W.S. CONGER."

Cobourg, January 4, 1842.

— — The Cobourg Star, January 5, 1842.

XI/A COLLECTION OF ITEMS
1837-1848

As reflected in the Cobourg Star newspaper of given date.

For this section, the author has assembled a series of short newspaper items with the hope they will make for added interest, and at the same time, inform and record some small events that helped to make up the day by day occurrences in Cobourg, at the time as dated.

Queen's College

NOTICE - A Public Meeting of Presbyterians and other inhabitants of Cobourg and its vicinity, favourable to the erection of the University of Queen's College at Kingston, will be held in St. Andrew's Church, Cobourg, on Tuesday, the 4th day of February next, at 11 o'clock in the forenoon, for the purpose of adopting such measures as will best promote this great object.

The meeting will be addressed by several ministers and laymen. Cobourg, 21st January, 1840.

— — January 22, 1840.

Queen's College — An Editorial

Having been unavoidably prevented by public duties from attending the meeting held yesterday, in St. Andrew's Church, in promotion of this projected institution, we are unable to present our readers with the particulars this week, but are promised an account for our next number. We are happy to understand that the meeting was very numerously attended, and its object supported with unprecedented spirit and success, as the subscription entered into on the occasion will abundantly testify — — for it amounted to the munificent sum of three hundred and twenty pounds.

— — February 5, 1840

THE CHURCH — We are happy to announce, that a weekly religious paper under this title, in connection with the Church of England, will shortly be issued from this office.

— — April 19, 1837

We are truly gratified to hear that the Reverend Egerton Ryerson has arrived in Toronto from England, having succeeded, it is said, at legth in obtaining a grant of 4,100 pounds in aid of the Upper Canada Academy in this town. This institution under its present and excellent and judicious management, is fast and justly gaining ground in the estimation of the public.

— — June 21, 1837

GLOBE NEWSPAPER — The undermentioned having determined to close his business immediately with the view of returning to England early in the ensuing Spring, hereby calls on all persons indebted to the GLOBE NEWSPAPER, lately published in Cobourg, to make payments to him of their respective debts, on or before the first of February.

ALFRED RUBIDGE
— — January 3, 1838

NOTICE — The undersigned, Blacksmiths of Cobourg and vicinity, give notice that, in consequence of hard times, they have come to the resolution of closing all credit business; and that from and after the first day of February next, all work done by any of them must be settled for in cash or otherwise, on delivery.

MATTHEW PURSER   GEORGE EDGECOMBE   THOMAS RATCLIFF
ALEX BROWN   RICHARD SOLOMON
GEORGE HAMILTON   JOHN CONNELL

— — January 31, 1838

SOAP and CANDLE MANUFACTORY — — The subscriber begs to inform his friends and the public generally, that he has removed his establishment to Orange Street, near Mr. Weller's Coach factory.

William Hitchens
— — July 4, 1838

Re: PLANTING of TREES in towns.

"For your streets, I recommend the alternate planting out of Rock Maples, Elms, White Ash, White Maple, Basswood, Beech and Red, White and other Oaks. The Rock Maple is certainly one of our most superb trees.

An article.
— — August 22, 1838

MR. BENJAMIN THROOP, who has conducted a retail business since about 1820 at the S.W. Corner of King and Division Streets announces he has sold out his stock in trade, and rented his store to Mr. J.E. Tremain.

— — November 22, 1838

COBOURG IRON and BRASS FOUNDRY — advertises a variety of Iron, Brass and Machine Work. Machinery for Grist, Saw Mill and Machinery castings.

J. McLenhan & Co.
— — March 20, 1839

WOOL CARDING — The subscriber has taken for a term of years, the well known stand at Mr. George Ham's Mill, where he is ready to do any work in his line of business at short notice.

C. PERRY, Clothier
— — May 15, 1839

SETTLERS ARRIVE — We had yesterday morning the gratification of welcoming back to Cobourg Lieutenant Rubidge, R.N. after an absence in England of nearly two years. Mr. Rubidge brings with him near two hundred stout, healthy and loyal emigrants (Irish) to our population.

— — July 10, 1839

THE DIFFERENCE — with reference to the plan to raid Cobourg late in July of 1839.

In the month of December, 1837 the news of Toronto being invested with a rebel force reached the Town of Cobourg, late on the night of Tuesday the 5th.

On the morning of Thursday the 7th, every loyal man in the neighbourhood was under arms and on the march.

On Sunday morning the 10th, near two thousand men from the Newcastle District, ready to shed their last drop of blood in defence of the British Crown, entered the City of Toronto.

On the following day, the 11th, several of those noble fellows went over as volunteers to the Niagara Frontier, and remained there till Navy Island was evacuated, a period of six weeks.

When the Newcastle Volunteers thus marched 72 miles in three days, the roads were almost impassable; and on their arrival in the city most of them were nearly exhausted, the blood gushing from their feet, and the physical suffering of all was intense.

On the 29th of July, 1839, the Cobourg plot was discovered.

On the 30th, the government received intelligence of it.

On the 1st of August, the Magistrates of the town addressed a letter to His Excellency that there was a real apprehension of open and secret violence, and a renewal of American sympathy on a large scale, and requesting immediate and effective protection.

On the 5th, finding this request unattended to, the Magistrates again, in still stronger language, addressed His Excellency.

On the 11th of August, nearly a fortnight after the discovery of the plot, one company of Militia, consisting of 80 men, rank anf file, reached Cobourg.

In December, 1837, it took two thousand men three days to march 72 miles over winter roads, through rebel settlements, and in constant expectation of attack.

In August, 1839, it takes the Government at least one week to despatch a single Company of Militia by steam boat, after two pressing representations from the Magistrates. We leave these facts to speak for themselves.

— — August 14, 1839

The Newcastle Turf Club was active in Cobourg from 1841 to 1844.

JAMES GRAY BETHUNE ESTATE — — We have learned with much pleasure, and from good authority, that the long pending and vexatious chancery suit between the late James Gray Bethune, Esq., and the Bank of Upper Canada, has been adjusted, and finally settled by arbitration. The arrangement it appears, will give the Bank Directors some valuable property at Peterborough with good title, while it awards and secures to Col. Covert, one of the plaintiffs in the suit, all those valuable and well situated lots of land, in the centre of the Town of Cobourg, this fine property, hitherto tied up, and unserviceable, will now be brought to market, and means afforded to the enterprising community, to fill up that great vacuum, opposite the Town Hall and Market Place, with handsome houses, in most elevated and best part of Cobourg.

— — August 17, 1842

A special census of Upper Canada was ordered by the government in 1842. Newspaper comment is of interest.

We now proceed to give a summary of the Census, taking both the Assessment and the special census return. We fear that the latter is very imperfect and cannot be relied upon as to particulars. It may, however give some statistics of the District, and we are sure in most cases the return is under rather than over the truth.

— — February 22, 1843

NOTICE — All persons indebted to the estate of the late George Ham, are requested to make immediate payment of their respective accounts, and those having claims against the said estate, will please present them, duly attested, to the undersigned for liquidation.

N.G. HAM, Administrator
— — April 19, 1843

TO RENT — FOR ONE YEAR — — The Ontario Mills, Cobourg, so well known, situated near the town, and to the harbour here, having three run of stones in good order, with a small dwelling house for the miller. Also the distillery, capable of running 30 to 40 bushels of grain each day. The distillery is in excellent order, and in every way complete, and attached to it are extensive and convenient hog pens, with a small dwelling house for the distiller.

Apply to — James McCutcheon, Esq., Toronto; D'Arcy E. Boulton, esq.; Shaw Armour, Land Agent, Cobourg.

— — May 29, 1844

MAP OF COBOURG — Few things are of more importance in a large and growing commercial town, where every foot of land is daily increasing in value, than a good map, defining clearly the boundary of every separate lot and street, and the correctness of which may be relied upon. Such a decideratum we are glad to say, is now forthcoming for the Town of Cobourg. Mr. W.G. Crofton, Esq., (Former teacher) and late editor of this paper having in addition to his already announced map of the Colborne and Newcastle Districts, which is nearly ready for issue, just completed for publication in Lithograph a very useful and much wanted plan of the Corporation limits, taking in the Court House, Hamilton Mills, etc. It is now in course of subscription. (Added Note — This in all probability was the first composite plan of the Town of Cobourg. No copy has been available in recent years. Sir Sanford Fleming's Map of Cobourg, issued in November of 1847, is available at the Dominion Archives, Ottawa — P.L.C.)

— — The Cobourg Star, June 4, 1845

STEAM-BOAT COBOURG, For Sale. — Public notice is hereby given, that the Steam-Boat COBOURG, with engines, furniture, etc. as she now lies, will be sold by auction (if not previously disposed of by private sale) on Monday the 1st day of February, next, at 12 o'clock, at Brown's Wharf. The above boat is propelled by two low pressure engines, of 50 horse power each, which are in good order.

By Order of the Committee,
David M. Patterson, Secretary

Toronto, 9th of November, 1840.

— — November 18, 1840

HARBOUR COMPANY's OFFICE, Cobourg, April 5, 1841. — Notice is hereby given, that tenders will be received by this office, until the 15th day of the current month, from persons willing to undertake to construct and put out not less than six cribs (And more if required) at the southern extremity of the western pier. For particulars, apply to the undersigned.

W.H. KITTSON, Secretary
— — April 7, 1841

EDITORIAL — We perceive that the Harbour Company are actively engaged in getting in timber to complete the wharf. They have removed the store house from its former position (on Division Street) and placed it at the west side of the pier.

Mr. Kittson has laid down the keel of a large boat, to be propelled on Ericson's Principle, and which is to proceed direct to Montreal and return by way of the Rideau. She is expected to be ready about the first of June.

We also hear it is intended to commence two other schooners. Give us but some good communication with the back townships and our trade must flourish.

— — February 23, 1842

EDITORIAL — Cobourg is beginning to assume an air of business that is highly gratifying. Several new houses are being put up, some of them of a very superior class. The keel of a schooner of large dimensions has been laid down, our hotels are crowded with immigrants, very many of them being persons of capital.

— — June 1st, 1842

IMPROVEMENTS — We are delighted to perceive the rapid emprovements which are being made in this good town of Cobourg. Several excellent houses are being built, the Corporation is busy laying down side-walks, the Harbour Company have in their employment several men perfecting the laying out of cribs to complete the harbour, everything looks like business. Well do the people of Cobourg merit success, and sincerely do we congratulate them on the present appearance of the town. The subject is so tempting as almost to entince us to say more but for this week we must conclude.

— — July 20, 1842

LAUNCH — Yesterday afternoon, a fine schooner built for Mr. Foley, was launched. She is a good specimen of naval architecture, and does credit to her builder, Mr. Collins. We were not present at the launch but we have heard that "she glided gracefully into her native element."

— — September 14, 1842

PORT OF COBOURG — — We have been furnished with the following table of the imports and exports at the Port of Cobourg during the year 1841.

87 barrels of apples; 54 barrels of ashes; 112 barrels of beaf; 417 firkins of butter; 30 tops of bran; 134 barrels of beer; 4 carriages; 1793 bushels of corn; 2 barrels of fish; 18,000 barrels of flour; 140,000 feet of lumber; 51 barrels of lard; 560 tons of mdse.; 278 barrels of meal; 1823 barrels of pork; 593 bushels of peas; 389 dozen pails; 635 barrels of plaster; 3018 barrels of salt; 1002 barrels of whiskey; 7,914 bushels of wheat; 3,664 cords of wood; 50,000 staves;

There were 597 vessels over 50 tons burthen; 73 vessels under 50 tons burthen touched this port during the season.

— — April 27, 1842

NOTICE — A dividend of six pounds on each share in the Steamer COBOURG has been this day declared, and will be paid after this date, at the office of Messers Gamble & Boulton, Toronto.

CLARKE GAMBLE, Chairman
April 9, 1842
— — May 11, 1842

THE DUTIES COLLECTED at the Port of Cobourg, during the year 1842, amounted to 1,076 Pounds, 14s. 3½d.; and the value of goods imported and not subject to duty is 4,323 pounds 17s.

— — February 8, 1843

COBOURG IMPROVEMENTS — Part of an Editorial. — — . . . Within four years its appearance has been totally changed, and few who visited it earlier than 1838, could not now know it as the same place. During the last year some 50 substantial buildings have been put up and preparations are being made for much more extensive operations during the coming summer, and what, but a few years ago appeared as chimneys, have now every likelihood of being perfected, that the whole incorporated space of Cobourg will, in a comparatively short time, be covered with buildings.

We read some time since in a Bath journal, of a plan adopted in that city, which was a selection of a committee to supervise public improvement, and which plan had been attended to with great success. Now there are two or three things which in this town are very desirable, and which judging from the unanimity that has hitherto existed on all questions of local interest, we make no doubt might easily be accomplished, we shall merely name them, leaving it to others to take up the matter and discuss it fully.

 First — The erection of a Town Hall.

 Second — Opening the Market Place to the lake.

 Third — Procuring some ground for a public square.

 Fourth-Making some improvement in the neighbourhood of the Wharf.

— — January 17, 1844

COMMON SCHOOL TEACHERS — The Board of Police of this Town, will on Monday next, the 8th instant, at 10 o'clock, A.M. in the Town Hall receive applications from such teachers as may be desirous of being appointed to any of the Common Schools within the Corporation.

A board of Examiners will be in attendance to examine as to the qualifications and characters of the applicants.

DAVID BRODIE, Police Clerk
Town Hall, Cobourg, 1st May, 1843
— — May 3, 1843

EDITORIAL

Ater a winter almost unprecedented in length and severity, indications of Spring begin to make their appearance, and never were they hailed with more delight by all classes; we have now had constant sleighing since the 28th of November (very nearly five months), and the consequence of this severity has been great suffering on the part of our farmers, whose supply of winter fodder is quite exhausted, and whose cattle suffer greviously; hay is scare and brings most exhorbitant prices, we have heard of 18 and 20 dollars per ton being asked.

— — April 5, 1843

We mentioned a short time ago, that J. Calcutt, Esq., was erecting a steam mill. It is now in full operation, producing flour equal, if not superior to any mill in the country.

— — February 21, 1844

COBOURG and TORONTO — It is generally allowed that few men have shown a greater degree of public spirit, or more anxious readiness to meet the general wish than Mr. Weller. We have now to notice an additional proof of the truth of these remarks; Mr. Weller has started a daily line of stages between this town and Toronto, by which an opportunity will be given to travellers to see some of the finest townships in the Province; these coaches start from both places every morning at 7 o'clock, and arrive at their destination early in the evening. Fare through, $2.00.

— — May 8, 1844

We would call attention to the Board of Police to the state of the bridge on the road to the Court House. By timely repairs, great inconvenience and expense may be avoided.

— — May 22, 1844

NOTICE — Tenders will be received till the 22nd of March at the office of Mr. Wallace, Ontario Mills, Cobourg, for the construction of a dam across the stream opposite the Roman Catholic Church. (Note: William Street location.)

Plans and specifications to be seen at the office of Mr. Wallace. Tenders will be opened on Saturday, 29th instant, at 2 o'clock. Security will be required for the performance of the contract.

— — March 11, 1845

(Added note: This dam was of timber construction, with heavy plank facing and anchored behind two timber, rock-filled cribs in mid stream. The dam remained in position for over 100 years, and in the 20th Century was known as the 'Dye Works Dam'. The pond created backed up water beyond the junction of the two main streams. The writer often fished in the pond, swam in the water and skated on the pond's ice.P.L.C.)

COMMERCIAL — The imports to Cobourg this year are very extensive, all kinds of goods are in profusion, and some of the selections evince a growing taste for the luxuries of life, springing from increasing prosperity. Our merchants' shops offer displays not inferior to those of Toronto or Montreal.

Messers Wallace and MacKechnie's Woolen Factory is in a forward state, and the liberal terms on which they deal with the farmers for their wool, and the encouragement they held out to the cultivation of superior breeds will soon work their sure effects.

— — June 18, 1845

Editorial — In directing the attention of the travelling community to the advertisement in a subsequent column, of Mr. R. SINCLAIR, of the GLOBE HOTEL in this town, announcing the opening of that truly splendid new establishment, it is no more than a matter of strict duty to declare, in justice to the individual and with due regard for the public interest, that it is in every respect a house of very superior standing, for elegance and appointment, comfort and accomodation, not to be surpassed we would say certainly, if equalled, in Canada West, and we very much doubt if we may also include Montreal.

— — September 10, 1845

EARLY CLOSING — We, the undersigned Merchants of Cobourg, willing at all times to comply with the request of our Clerks, and desirous to extend to them the same privilege as that enjoyed by others in similar capacities in Montreal, Kingston and Toronto, do hereby agree to close our respective places of business at 7 o'clock in the evening, from Monday the 22nd of December, until the end of April.

Macbean & Strong	A. Jeffrey	William Boyer
J.F. Hurst	Easton and Wright	Thomas Eyre
John Field	J. Calcutt, Jr.	G.A. Nixon
L.F. Brook	Peter Morgan	J.S. Beamish
Goodeve & Corrigal	J. Vance Boswell & Co.	F. Logan per W. Beatie
John Kennedy	Graveley and Jackson	Henry Terry
James Hey	George Boyer	James Tremaine

Benjamin Clark, Esq., and W. Tremain, Esq., two of our leading merchants, being absent from home, their names do not appear in the above, but they are understood to be entirely in favor of the arrangement, and will doubtless sign it on their return.

— — December 17, 1845

FLEMING's Map of Cobourg — By advertisement in to-day's paper it will be seen that Fleming's Map is now ready for delivery. It is decidedly the best work of art of its kind that has ever been executed in Canada, and reflects the highest possible credit on the artists who did it. We are sure that no inhabitant of Cobourg will be so heedless of the progress of his town, as to refuse to buy a work which so faithfully sets her advantages, natural and acquired, before the public.

— — November 17, 1847

FLEMING'S MAP OF THE TOWN OF COBOURG (Advertisement)
The above plan from a late survey made by order of the Board of Police, on a scale five chains to an inch, is now lithographed and ready for delivery at the Town Hall.

Price, from 7s 6d to Four Dollars.
Cobourg November 16, 1847.

— — November 17, 1847

GRAVEL ROADS — We have been literally besieged in our office by complaints against the heavy tolls on our roads. We would earnestly recommend the Directors of the Port Hope and Cobourg line to take off their gates for a couple of months till the road be somewhat packed. The Grafton Road is infinitely before the other, but the toll is too high at present, as is also the case on the Rice Lake road.

— — November 8, 1848

WILLIAM WELLER

William Weller, the stage coach king and a long time resident of Cobourg, was an active person in various endeavors. He served nine times on the elective Cobourg Board of Police, two of those terms as President. When municipal councils were formed in 1850, Weller again served eight times, three of those terms as Mayor. He died as Mayor of Cobourg in 1863. He also served on the District Council when it was first set up in 1842. In the latter part of the year 1847, William Weller contested the election for the Union Legislature of the United Canadas in the riding of South Northumberland. In this contest Weller was not elected due to party politics carrying the day. His appeal to the Electors of South Northumberland is very interesting and informative. The appeal follows:

"TO THE ELECTORS OF SOUTH NORTHUMBERLAND
"Gentlemen:

"At the solicitation of several individuals from different parts of this District, I am induced to come forward and offer myself, at the ensuing General Election, as a candidate for your representation in the Legislature of this Province.

"This step, gentlemen, is not prompted by any mercenary motives, I am known personally to the most of you, and it is for you to decide whether, from character of circumstances, I have interests to gratify that are at variance with yours, or prejudicial to those of the Colony at large.

"I have resided among your for many a long year — — for the greater part of my life; and I trust that during that period, I have not been found wanting in those duties and observances which constitute a good citizen, and a faithful subject. True, it may be urged that I have not had the honour of being born under the British Flag, but then, gentlemen, my sons and daughters were born under it. It has become mine by adoption and choice; and, let it be remembered, that in the hour of danger I was found at my post in its defence.

"Here, and in this very District too, are all that are near and dear to me — — my property, which is of some value, lies here intermingled with your own; proving our interests to be inseparable. Whatever affects your welfare affects mine. You cannot prosper without my participating in your prosperity, or suffer without my sharing your adversity; and as I am no needy office seeker, who is ready to sell you at a moment's notice, you have at least presumptive evidence of the honesty of my intentions.

"In politics I am "Wheat at a dollar a bushel and good roads to your doors". Who, I wish to enquire, can do justice and follow the humbugging system of the day? Who can call himself an independent man and pledge himself to support every measure, whether good or bad, that may be introduced to the House by the leader of this Administration or of that Administration? No individual in existance, gentlemen; and sooner than purchase the suffrage of any constituancy on such terms as these, I would deliberately and cheerfully forgo the honour of representing it, were it even accorded to me by acclamation.

"Gentlemen, I care not a farthing for party politics, my text is, and ever shall be, sustain the Constitution throughout all its bearings — — strengthen the link that binds us to the Mother Country — — improve the conditions of the farmer, who is the bone and sinew of the Province — — proscribe no body of men through the enactment of repressive laws and irrespective of party, encourage education through the length and breadth of the land.

"And now, gentlemen, having laid this brief statement before you, I shall conclude my remarking, that, did time permit, it would give me sincere pleasure to visit you all individually; but as the election will take place in a very few days, I am of course deprived of that gratification. However, if you consider an individual who is of necessity deeply interested in the welfare of this District — — one who has handled the scythe and plough for many a day himself — — worthy of the highest trust which is your gift, most heartily do place my humble abilities at your service.

I am, gentlemen, Yours sincerely,
WILLIAM WELLER

COBOURG, December 7th, 1847

XII/THE FLOURISHING FORTIES

The Cobourg Board of Trade

A Board of Trade was first organized in Cobourg in September of 1837, as reported earlier in this history. How long that organization functioned, and what it accomplished we do not know. Apparently it became defunct. Now, a second Board of Trade is under organization as reported in the Cobourg Star:

For the Cobourg Star,

At a meeting of the Merchants held this day pursuant to notice published by a committee appointed at a preliminary meeting, held in Mr. Tremain's office, on Monday the 1st, instant, for the purpose of taking into consideration the propriety of forming a Board of Trade in and for the Town of Cobourg; E. Perry, Esq., having been called to the chair and T. Evans, Esq., appointed Secretary, it was —

RESOLVED, 1st. — That this meeting being aware of the advantages likely to arise from having the general business of the Town under the supervision of a body of men, whose education, habits, and experience fit them for such duties, deem it expedient to form a Board of Trade in and for the Town of Cobourg and vicinity.

RESOLVED, 2nd. — That the Constitution now read, being a modification of that which governs a similar body in Toronto, be adopted as the constitution of the Cobourg Board of Trade.

RESOLVED, 3d — That such gentlemen as are present this evening, (being merchants, and feeling disposed to subscribe to the Constitution) do form themselves into a Board of Trade, the same to go into immediate effect provided fifteen names be subscribed.

RESOLVED, 4th — That as soon as the above number of fifteen subscribers be complete, they proceed to elect a President, Vice President, and Secretary, together with a Committee of Management for the coming year.

RESOLVED, 5th — That as many gentlemen who were expected to have been present at this meeting, have not attended; and in order to allow them the opportunity of becoming members without the test of the ballot, that all such qualified persons as shall subscribe to the Constitution within one week shall be admitted members.

The requisite number being present, and having duly subscribed to the Constitution, proceeded to the election of officers and organization of the Board, when the following gentlemen were duly elected, viz:

BOARD of TRADE

Charles H. Morgan, Esq., President
W. Tremain, Esq., Vice President

COMMITTEE:

Peter Morgan	S.E. MacKechnie	G.M. Goodeve
E. Perry	Thomas Evans	G. Boyer
A. Jeffrey	John Wallace	J. McCarty
B. Clarke	H. Terry	
W. VanIngen.	W. Strong	

The Committee being formed, appointed Mr. T. Evans to act as Secretary and Treasurer for the ensuing year.

Charles H. Morgan, Esq., having taken the the chair, the thanks of the meeting was voted to E. Perry, Esq., for his impartial and efficient conduct therein.

signed Charles H. Morgan, President
Thomas Evans, Secretary and Treasurer

Cobourg September 8th, 1845

— — The Cobourg Star, September 17, 1845

At a meeting of the Board of Trade in this town, it was resolved that a Reading Room should be established, to be called "THE COBOURG COMMERCIAL READING ROOM.", and that as soon as a sufficient number of subscribers could be obtained, steps should be taken to carry the above object into effect; a committee was forthwith appointed, who having obtained the requisite number of names, called a general meeting of subscribers for Friday the 12th Instant, when the following gentlemen were elected as Committee of Management. (Ten names follow, A. Jeffrey was elected President.)

Cobourg, 15th September, 1845.

— — The Cobourg Star, September 17, 1845

The Cobourg Curling Club

The Cobourg Curling Club has been active for a long time. In fact, the start was made away back in 1845, and the Cobourg Star newspaper of December 3, confirms this.

CURLING CLUB — We are requested to give notice that a meeting will be held at the Globe Hotel, on Friday Evening next, at 8 o'clock, another indication of the growing spirit of the Town of Cobourg, and harmony as colonists and foster a feeling of loyal attachment to the institutions of the Mother Country than the introduction of these national games."

The Club was activated, and for a start they had no covered rink, artificial ice was something of which members had no knowledge, and the wide outdoor was their place to play the game. What sportsmen they were! Notice the following:

"CURLING CLUB — We are requested to give notice that a match between the Bachelors and the Married members of this Club, for beef and greens, is appointed to take place on WALLACE'S POND, to-morrow at half past one o'clock, P.M."

> — The Cobourg Star, January 14, 1846.
> (Note: Wallace's Pond was part of the Factory Creek and to the north of King Street.)

The Cobourg Star failed to report on who paid for the beef and greens, but become further informed by reading this note by the editor in his February 11th issue:

"CURLING — Our Curling Club proceeds rapidly, having had several days of excellent play; and we hope that when next winter comes they will be prepared to extend their operations by showing their skill to some other of their Curling friends. This game appears to us to be one requiring great judgment, long practise, and more than ordinary bodily strength. It is in fact the cricket of winter, and we are rejoiced to see it becoming so general. We have been handed the following by a member, there is no need to say he is one of the Benedicts. It is invidious in those "more fortunate" to twit their antagonists with their misfortunes."

CURLING — On Friday evening last one of the most keenly contested matches which has yet been played by the Cobourg Curlers, came off between four of the Married and an equal number of the Single members.

The game was played by moonlight, and as the result will show, was carried on in a manner which would do credit to older and more practised club. The Benedicts were, in this instance, as indeed generally the case, victorious, still, considering the smallness of the odds and the length of the struggle, we almost feel inclined to recommend the Bachelors again to take the field against perhaps in every respect their more fortunate opponents.

The following is the score of the game:

SINGLE		MARRIED	
Paton	5	Bertram	12
Wilson	6	Cameron	13
Murray	12	Kittson	4
Buck, Skip	13	Weller, Skip	12
	36		41

Time — Two Hours and a Half.

> — The Cobourg Star, February 11, 1846

James Gray Bethune

In a property deed, dated the 20th of September, 1817, James (Gray) Bethune is named as a merchant of Kingston, and Robert Henry as a Merchant of Montreal. The two had purchased some 203 acres of land in the western part of Cobourg, namely Lot Number 20, of Hamilton Township, which included a water-power site and industry. The price paid was 1,500 pounds.

By the 26th of April, 1818, Bethune sold out his holdings, his share, in the above industrial property to his partner, Mr. Henry for 500 Pounds. This deed records him as a resident of the Township of Hamilton, a merchant of the firm, Robert Henry and Bethune. These records tell us that both of these gentlemen had moved to Cobourg by early 1818, and established a local retail business. Bethune was twenty-four years of age at the time of his arrival.

Cobourg was but a hamlet in the year 1818. John Monjeau was already retailing merchandise on King Street. Elijah Buck, Dr. Timothy Kittridge, James Williams, Ebenezer Perry and others were entrepreneurs. Bethune was young, venturesome, opportunistic, ambitious and possessed drive. As the small village grew, so did Bethune in his business ventures. He is reported as Cobourg's first Postmaster. By 1825, he was involved in town property deals as agent of Cobourg's first plan of Subdivision. He was a big promoter in the initial development of the Cobourg Harbour, His business transactions including the importing of goods, and the exporting of farm products. He held rank in the Militia and married into a wealthy, well placed family, the Coverts. He became an Agent for the Bank of Upper Canada and Cobourg land agent for the Canada Company.

Bethune was a planner with an imaginative insight. He saw the need of the Cobourg Harbour as a utility for exporting the products of the hinterland to the north, and coupled with this need, transportation facilities to bring the wealth of the north through Cobourg. Adept at promotion, he became involved with boat activities on Rice Lake, in addition to the promoting the building of the Steam-boat, "Cobourg". He had other inland business ventures. In the larger sphere, he had connections with powerful people in Montreal and Toronto. He became the 'kingpin' at the centre of Cobourg's developing commercial system.

Unfortunately for himself and for Cobourg, he was weak in looking after the day to day details and in areas of management. He overextended his activities, and made some false moves in money management, extended too much credit, and started to flounder in the financial waters, which finally engulfed him and took him under. He became a bankrupt.

James Gray Bethune was interested in the Cobourg Railway Company idea, but by the time that Company was organized in 1835, he was unable to assist with its promotion. Had it been otherwise, as in the case of the Cobourg Harbour Company, the project may have gone ahead in 1835, and capitalized on the early development to the north. The delays and the hesitations of the Directors of the railroad in 1835 and 1836 interfered with actual construction, which did not materialize until 1852. By that time there was strong competition in other places, particularly in Port Hope, for the trade of the northern townships.

The Cobourg Harbour Company

Bethune owned a large block of stock in both the Cobourg Harbour Company and the Cobourg Steam-boat Company. At the time of his financial collapse, these shares were acquired by outside interests, especially wealthy people living in Toronto. The balance of voting stock in both Companies, moved from Cobourg to Toronto. The Cobourg merchants thus lost control of the operation of the Steam-boat "Cobourg".

The Cobourg Harbour Company prospered, and the revenue brought in a nice financial return to the stockholders each year after 1832. The controling interests, outside of Cobourg, were only concerned with the profits, and cared less for the necessary repairs to piers and the general maintenance of the harbour. From the year 1836 on, the piers were deteriorating and wave-washed sand reduced the depth of the harbour basin. The Rebellion of 1837, and its after-math left a tight money market. By the early 1840's the harbour was in a run-down condition, yet it produced profits for the stockholders.

In 1841, there was a revival of interest in the making of improvements to the harbour, and in finishing the necessary extension to the then western pier, in order to retard the movement of sand into the basin by westerly storms. The Harbour Company advertised for contractors to supply material, build timber cribs, and set in place six or more of these cribs. Preparations for this work were moving along in the Spring of 1842.

The new Union Government of Canada, in 1841, established a department bearing the title "Board of Works." In the summer of 1842, the Cobourg Harbour Company, for reasons unknown, entered into an assignment agreement with this government body to complete the harbour. The work involved pier construction and the dredging of the basin, at an estimated cost of 4,240 Pounds. The Board of Works took possession of the harbour, and the Company had no say in directing the work. The writer made a search for a copy of this Indenture agreement in both the Cobourg Registry Office and the Archives of Ontario without any success in locating the document or learning the details of its contents. The terms of takeover remain vague.

The work of improving and finishing the Cobourg Harbour was contracted out to a Mr. Russell in the amount of 5,413 Pounds 3s 7d. The accumulation of timber and material collected by the Harbour Company was turned over for the use of Mr. Russell.

Cribs were built and installed at the end of the then western pier in 1842 and 1843. According to a report, some older cribs were found to be falling appart and these were repaired. There was some extra work done by the contractor.

Communications between the Board of Works and the Harbour Company left much to be desired. Company Directors and officials were often ignored as to costs and other business matters. The dredging of the harbour basin was not performed. The accumulation of sand was creating a danger for shipping. There were also outside adverse interferences with the Cobourg harbour, particularly from Port Hope. In spite of protests, the Company made very little progress in their dealings with the Board of Works.

It was found out much later that Mr. Russell had been paid some 10,000 pounds for his work with no explanation forthcoming to the Company, yet they were saddled with this debt and interest charges. Some Cobourg people were of the opinion that Mr. Russell had received double pay. The Government refused to make an investigation, and according to the Cobourg Star newspaper, the whole affair was hushed up.

The citizens of Cobourg held an indignation meeting as late as March 10th, 1848, and reviewed the whole affair. Even by that time, the harbour basin had not been dredged, in spite of some 500 pounds being set aside by the government for that specific purpose some two or three years earlier. It all appears like a piece of messy business with some dirty politics playing a part. The Harbour Company ended up with the 10,000 Pounds of debt and the basin was left undredged. One bright fact remains, the annual revenue had increased beyond the 1,200 Pounds figure.

The petition that was prepared in 1848, by the townspeople for the Legislature was too late as the sessions came to an end. The stockholders were the losers in this affair. The agreement signed in 1842, apparently, prevented the Company from doing the dredge work on their own initiative.

West End Industry

Jones' Creek, Cobourg Brook, or the Factory Creek, located in the western part of Cobourg, has been the site for water-powered industry from early in the 19th century and later for steam-powered industry down to these later days. In earlier years, its water power motivated a great variety of saw-mills, grist-mills, distilleries, and manufactories located throughout its main stream and branches, from the high waters of Lake Ontario into the high hills of Hamilton Township. We review here the story of industry located in the western part of Cobourg, namely Township Lot Number twenty, in Concession "A".

Elias Jones, the first settler to own lots nineteen and twenty, retained the first for twenty years, but sold the second in December of 1803 to John Nugen, except for two and a half acres at the lakefront. Early stories report that a sawmill was placed in operation on this stream, and it is believed Nugen erected the dam some 200 feet above King Street for this mill. Nugen sold out to his father-in-law, William Carson, in 1805, the 215 acres, and the following year Carson sold the property to Donald MacDonald of Kingston for 547 Pounds.

The MacDonald family retained the property for over eleven years. It is believed that during this time a grist mill was added at the dam site.

In June of 1817 MacDonald's son, Alexander, sold off six acres, located at the corner of Burnham and Elgin Street to Lewis Stiles, who erected a hotel and became part of the Village of Amherst. Another sale of six acres adjacent to the Stiles purchase went to Mark Burnham, thus reducing the property by twelve acres, at the north end.

In September of 1817. Alexander MacDonald sold the remaining 203 acres to Robert Henry and James Gray Bethune for 1,500 Pounds. In a few months Bethune sold his share to Henry, who retained the property for fourteen years. It is believed that during this time, Robert Henry built the large, lovely, rectangular dwelling to the west of and overlooking the dam and millpond, known as "TORBECH", and used this house as his dwelling. This building remained for over one hundred years. In addition, Robert Henry maintained a farming operation. The higher ground to the west of the creek was of a fertile, black loam soil, excellent for growing a variety of crops and garden vegetables.

On the 14th of July, 1831, Robert Henry sold his west end propery to Mr. George Ham, of the Village of Bath. The sale included 203 acres of land, the dam and mill-pond with its attached industries, plus goods, chattels, farming utensils, etc., at a price of 6,000 pounds. George Ham took up residence in "TORBECH". He was active in the militia, served two years on the Board of Police, and took an interest in local developmets. He died suddenly on the 7th of February, 1843, at the age of 48 years.

Mr. George Ham was indebted to the Hon. Peter McGill with a mortgage on the property. McGill took possession in January of 1844. In September of that same year he sold the property to Mr. Stuart E. MacKechnie, who appointed Mr. Patrick Wallace to be his administrative attorney. Wallace took up residence in TORBECH.

Changes were in progress soon after MacKechnie and Wallace came into possession of their west end property. Much of the land on the higher ground was sub-divided into town lots and streets. MacKechnie was an active industrialist and he proceeded at once to build a large woolen mill in the valley to the south of King Street. The large brick structure was for a number of years powered by water, conducted in a five foot wooden enclosed flume leading from the dam site, under King Street to the basement of the new building, some 400 feet long. Here an ultra modern water wheel was installed that powered the machinery of the mill. In later years, water power was replaced by steam power.

This woolen mill, at the time of its first operation, was the best of its kind in Upper Canada. The products were of excellent quality, and often took top prizes at competitive fairs. The writer recalls this mill in operation as a woolen industry in the year of 1913. In fact I once had a suit of clothes made from cloth manufactured in this mill. The industry was a great asset to Cobourg, and provided a good market for many farmers selling wool.

The Cobourg Star, of January 21st, 1846, gives a fine description of this new industry in the following story.

The Ontario Mills Woolen Factory

We have at length the pleasure of announcing that this establishment, the most extensive in British North America, is now in full operation. Of the benefits which it is destined to confer on the Newcastle District, setting aside its future important influence on the commerce of the Colony at large, there can be but one opinion, and we most heartily trust, that through the energetic support of all classes, it will realize to its patriotic proprietor, S.E. MACKECHNIE, Esq., that profitable return he is so well entitled to expect for his munificent expenditure of capital. We have had the pleasure afforded us of inspecting the whole establishment, and should be doing injustice to our feelings, were we to refrain from expressing our admiration of all details connected with it. The building substantially built of brick, is four stories and one half high, one hundred feet long and forty feet wide. In the ground story is located the magnificent water wheel, pronounced by all scientific men who have seen it, to be the finest ever constructed in this Province; also the fulling machinery, finishing room, and dye house. The second story is appropriated to the weaving department, a noble room running the whole length of the building, and supported by columns, where we had the pleasure of seeing that great invention of modern times, the Power Loom, in full operation. The third story is the Carding room, of the same dimension as the weaving room; and here curiosity is amply gratified in examining the delicate and complicated machinery by which the wool is prepared from its rough state, and fitted for being spun into yarn. The fourth story is the spinning room, also the whole length of the building, where Sir Richard Arkwright's wonderful invention, the Spinning Jenny, excites the admiration of the beholder. The upper or attic story, is appropriated for drying the wool after it having been washed and dyed. The building throughout is heated by steam, thus greatly diminishing the risk from fire, and the dying operations are performed by the same agent, in the most efficient manner: Altogether the Ontario Mills Woolen Factory is a most pleasant spectacle to look upon for all who feel an interest in the progressing advancement of Canada as a dependency of the British Crown, and from the activity and scientific skill of its operative Superintendent, as well as the enterprise of its worthy proprietor, we entertain no doubt of its future and rapid prosperity.

— The Cobourg Star, January 21, 1846

WOOL

The highest market price will be paid in Cash for WOOL, at the Ontario Mills Woolen Factory, Cobourg, by the Subscriber.

S.E. MACKECHNIE

Cobourg June 12, 1845

N.B. — Growers of Wool who may prefer it, will have an opportunity of exchanging any portion of their Wool for Cloth.

— — The Cobourg Star, February 4, 1846

List of Merchants, Mechanics, Etc., In The Town of Cobourg.
(As of January 1st, 1848)

Bakers and Confectioners
J. Hooey, T. Pratt, T. Elliott, J.C. Marshell

Butchers
J. Mann, O. Powell, — Plews, — Gerrans, — McKeown

Blacksmiths
M. Purser, W. Crosson, G. Edgecumbe, G. Hamilton, J. Robinson
P. Newton, W. Newton, W. Milne, J. Hawkins, J. Newton, J. Plunkett

Brewer
J. Calcutt

Bricklayers
W. Carveth, J. Clark

Cabinet Makers
F.S. Clench, George Russell, George Stephens, M.T. Hobart, Charltain & Huff

Coopers
L. Broughall, J. Young, S. Irwin, J. Tigh, J. Hutchinson

Carpenters and Builders
Messers Burnett, Messers Grieve, J. Canavan, W. Bradbeer, W. Pomeroy,
C. Pomeroy

Carriage Makers
A. Munson, J. McConnell, — Brewer, H. Stickles, W. Paine, — Simmons

Chandlers
W. Hitchins, , — Nixon

Distillers
J. Calcutt, P. Wallace, W.G. Scott

Engraver
J.D. Greenleaf

Founders
J. Helm & Son, — McLenhan

Gun Smith
W. Tobin

Hatters
A. Secor, P. Nihil

Millers
E. Perry & Co, J. Calcutt, J. White, P. Wallace

Marble Factory
S. Lewis

Painters & Glaziers
W.G. Hancock, J. Bain, S. Munro

Pump Maker
A. McAllister

Saddlers
— Averell, A. Halliday, Wm. Pearson, H. Hales, A. Hawkey

Smut Machine Makers
A. Duncan & Co.

Shoemakers
J. Hossack, J. Russell, J. Howard, J. Swain, J. Cuthbert, J. Pearce,
G. Thompson, H. Rundle, P. Beagan, — Noble, — McKinley, T. Judge,
— Noble, J. Armstrong, — McManus, — Kennedy

Tailors
P. McCallum, A. Milne, J. Holman, A. Frazer, H. Crosson, J. Croft, A. Paton,
D. Ross, R. Budge, W. Dumble

Tanners
N. Horton, , H. Boulter

Watchmakers
A. Pringle, , J. Nixon

Woolen Factory
S.E. McKechnie

Banks
Com. Bank of the Midland District, Bank of Montreal

Book Stores
F. House, , W. Boyder, Goodeve & Corrigal

Daguerrean Artist
G. Callender

Dentists
C. Poor, G. Callender

Drug Stores
H.H. Jackson, G. Boyer

Dry Goods Stores
E. Perry & Co., J. Field, J. McCarty, H. Terry, McBean & Strong
Goodeve & Corrigal, T. Harvey, J. Calcutt, J. Kennedy, J. Beamish
Gray & McLeod, Brooke & Beatty, W. Graveley, B. Clark

Grocery and Liquor Stores
J. Lockhead, J. Sutherland, J.McDonald

Hardware Stores
A. Jeffrey, J.F. Hurst, W. Van Ingen

Liquor Stores
P. Wallace, Campbell & Standley

Leather Store
N. Horton

Groceries
J. Guillet, J. Mitchell, J. Beatty, — Doney, W. Gilbard, P. Dobson, M.
McKenny

Recesses
Mrs. Armstrong, J. Butler, W. Alexander, — Derry

Hotel and Tavern Keepers
T. Duignan, J. Tennery, Hall & Saisbury, J. Thompson, W.H. Kells,
J. Connelly, J. McGran, J.L. Wilson, T. McMurtry, J. Lynn
E.C. Hull, W. Lawder

Lawyers
G.S. Boulton, Boulton & Cockburn, R.H. Throop, S. Smith, W.A. Garratt,
A. McDonald, R. Ruttan, J.M. Brodie

Doctors
J. Gilchrist, G. Goldstone, T. Holywell, J. Beatty, — Auston

The Queen's Birthday
"The 24th of May is the Queen's Birthday."

PROCLAMATION

THE BOARD of POLICE hereby recommend to the Loyal Inhabitants of the Town of Cobourg, that as Wednesday next, the
24th inst., is the Birth-Day of our beloved Queen, the same be
observed as a Holyday — — and that an ILLUMINATION take
place in the Evening, commencing at 8 o'clock, in honour of Her
Majesty — — recommendations with which, they doubt not, the
inhabitants will cheefrully comply.

The Board of Police also recommend that the Bells of the
Churches, College, Fire and other Public Bells be rung at 6
o'clock in the morning and at 8 o'clock in the evening, for at
least half an hour each time.
GOD SAVE THE QUEEN!!!
By order,

ASA A. BURNHAM,
President Board of Police

DAVID BRODIE,
Clerk of Police
Town Hall, Cobourg, 22 May, 1848
— — The Cobourg Star, May 24, 1848

The leadership given to this event by the President and Board of Police of
Cobourg, as stated in their Proclamation of the 22nd of May, 1848, produced
an occasion of rejoicing that is best described by the editor of the Cobourg Star
one week later in his May 31st issue. We are pleased to record his story.

HER MAJESTY'S BIRTH-DAY

Wednesday last, the Queen's Birth-day, was celebrated in this Town with great enthusiasm.

At an early hour a feu-de-joi was fired by everyone who could beg or borrow a fire-arm; the shop-roofs, hotels, and houses were decorated with British flags; the Fire Companies turned out in full trim; and all the bells of the Town rang out a merry peal.

During the day, extensive preparation was made for an illumination; fire-ball, serpents, wheels, torches, and innumerable other combustables, were got ready, including material for a huge bonfire.

At 8 in the evening the houses were lighted up, and a most brilliant and effective lighting up it was. The Factory, Victoria College, and the Court House, were the most consicuous objects; the Odd Fellows' and Orangemen's Halls were also magnificiently illuminated, but owing to the end windows only fronting the Town, they did not make so good a show. Of the Shops we admired Goodeve & Corrigal's which exhibited a very large transparency of a Crown and V.R. — The lights in Capt. Wallace's mansion were arranged with great taste, and so managed as to form numerous pleasing devices. Although many shops as well as private houses deserve particular mention, we have not space to indulge ourselves or our readers with a particular description. We must be content with saying that if the inhabitants had had a week's, instead of two day's notice, they could not have done the thing more effectively.

A little after 8, the Fire Companies formed a long Procession, each member having two torches fastened to four foot poles. They proceeded to the West end, and about nine lighted up, and commenced a serpentine walk through the town. This had a most pleasing and beautiful effect, and the Gallant Companies were cheered repeatedly by the hundreds of town and country folk who lined the sidewalk. On arriving opposite Division Street, Mr. W. Calcutt's battery of 13 guns fired a royal salute. About half-past 10 the procession ended, when rockets, fireworks, and bonfires were the order of the night.

By the bye, we must not forget to mention an excellent Band stationed on the roof of the Albion Hotel, which discoursed most eloquently. About 10 o'clock we left the scene of rejoicing, which, however, was not abandoned by many till a very late, or we should say, a very early, hour.

It is extremely gratifying for us to be able to say, that of the vast croud assembled in the streets on Wednesday night, we heard not one member of it who had acted improperly. All religions, all politics, all orders, had met to-gether for one great and noble object, that of paying honour to a beloved sovereign, and they were determined that no less holy, less patriotic feeling, should have a place in their hearts.

To this we can add

"GOD SAVE THE QUEEN"

We have been favoured with the following Abstract of the Census of the Town, by our esteemed Clerk of the Police, DAVID BRODIE, Esq.

Bakers 4	Emigrant Agents 1	Ministers 7
Butchers............4	Editors 3	Pump Makers 2
Brewers 2	Fishermen 4	Painters & Glaziers....5
Blacksmiths.........18	Female House	Post Masters 1
Book-Binders........1	Keepers 41	Professors...........4
Barristers 6	Farmers 7	Printers 4
Butlers 1	Fullers 2	Plasterers 6
Barbers.............4	Grocers............15	Revenue Inspector 1
Brick makers........2	Gentlemen 24	Surgeons & Physicians .5
Brick layers &	Gardeners 2	Shoemakers 31
Masons..........12	Gunsmiths 1	Sailors.............5
Booksellers...........1	Gaolers.............1	Schoolmasters 8
Bank Agents 2	Huntsman 1	Schoolmistresses 3
Bath keepers 1	Hatters 2	Sadlers 5
Cabinet Makers.......8	Harbour Masters......1	Students 4
Carriage Makers 5	Judge 1	Sheriff 1
Carpenters 42	Indian Supt 1	Surveyors 1
Clerks 9	Iron Finishers 1	Spinners 3
Collector of	Inn Keepers.........14	Stage Proprietors 1
Customs 1	Lath Splitters 1	Sculptors 1
Chandlers............2	Lime Burners 1	Tailors 10
Coopers 10	Land Agents 2	Tinsmiths............4
Chair Makers 2	Labourers 134	Tool Makers 1
Carters 2	Merchants 20	Teamster 3
Clothiers............1	Millers 3	Turners 1
Dyers 1	Merchant Tailors 3	Tanners 2
Dancing Masters 1	Mill Wrights 4	Waiters.............3
Druggists 2	Moulders 2	Weavers 3
Dress makers 3	Machine Makers 2	Watchmakers 2
Distillers............3	Machinists 2	
Cloth Finisher 1	Manufacturers........1	

CREEDS

Inhabitants at home..........3,444	Church of England...........1,342
On a journey, etc...............68	Church of Rome 567
3,512	Free Church, Presbyterian 627
	Others 5
Nation of England............627	Wesleyan Methodists 415
Nation of Scotland............282	Episcopal.....................79
Nation of Ireland.............950	Others 22
Of Canada French Origin 4	Baptists 15
of British 1,374	Independents (Congregational) ...51
Germany Holland 3	Quakers 5
United States 182	Denomination not named......162
Other Countries 22	No Creed.....................91
3,444	Not Accounted for............35
	3,444

— — — The Cobourg Star, August 9th, 1848.

Agricultural Societies

The Northumberland County Agricultural Society was first organized at Colborne in the year of 1828. This Society held four fairs, one at Colborne in 1829, one in 1830, and two in 1831. The Spring Fair and Cattle Show, of 1831, was held in Cobourg. The Society also gave prizes for two years for the best operated farms in the county. No fair was held in 1832, and the folowing year, it folded and became defunct.

Nearly four years later, the Society was revived under outstanding leadership. It slowly gained in strength and in the fall of 1839 again sponsored a fair and cattle show, this time at Grafton, and in conjunction with a newly formed Grafton Fair. The Society prospered, and followed through with fairs in each succeeding year.

In the year of 1843, the idea of organizing a Provincial Agricultural Association blossomed and finally materialized in 1846. The conception of staging a Provincial Fair took hold, and under hurried preparations, such an event was held in Toronto in October of that year. Under hurried circumstances, it may have been considered a success up to a point, but there were flaws in organization and in preparation. The initial start had been made, however, and plans went ahead for a fall Provincial Exhibition, to be held in Hamilton in 1847. The site chosen turned out to be a poorly a drained piece of ground. The day of the Fair, Jupiter Pluvious also attended, making the show grounds into a quagmire. In spite of the heavy rain, the Association's Annual Dinner was a big success, with the Governor General attending and delivering a most interesting and informative address. Financially, the organization lost money and acquired a debt, which had to be overcome later.

The active Northumberland Agricultural Society pressured the Executive of the Association to have the 1848 show held in their territory. The final decision as to location was in their favor, and the Town of Cobourg was selected as the site.

There were some very excellent and capable leaders in the Northumberland Society. They had staged very successful fairs in recent years, they had expertise and determination to make the 1848 event a success. With flaws and failings of the first two Provincial Exhibitions in their minds, and a debt to overcome, they set about early to prepare for the big event in the coming October. They laid through plans.

Some seven acres of ground, loaned by Mr. Patrick Wallace, was chosen for the fair in the west end of Cobourg. This field was to the north of King Street and between Burnham and Sinclair Streets. Here a slight ridge of ground, sloping away in every direction, provided for natural drainage in the event of rain.

A canvas was made of Agricultural Societies throughout the Province for prize money. Municipalities and others were asked for donations toward the cost of erecting fair buildings, etc. The Town of Cobourg gave 100 Pounds. The Newcastle District Council, serving an agricultural community, refused the request for a donation. The Agricultural Societies of Durham and Peterborough were very supportive with both money and manpower.

The seven acres were enclosed by a high board fence. Three main buildings were erected and subsidary structures arranged within the grounds. Cattle pens and judging parks were set up in a functional pattern. A large banquet hall was erected on the town market square. The Town even had a new bridge erected over the Factory Creek. Visitor accomodation was arranged for in hotels and in private homes. Cobourg went all out towards making this event a success.

By the last week of September, cattle men and display people commenced to arrive in Cobourg with their animals and their wares. Every lake boat, docking at the Cobourg Harbour, was loaded down to overcrowding. The exhibition was set for four days during the first week in October. The first two days of the fair were given over to assembling and judging, the last two for the visitors.

The Sunday and Monday previous to opening day produced a most violent type of storm with heavy rains and high winds throughout the Province. Lake Ontario generated such heavy seas that boats were unable to travel, let alone dock at the Cobourg Harbour. By Tuesday the storm abated, and exhibitors, though late, were able to get their displays set up. Judging too was delayed.

Fortunately, the visiting days were bright, sunny and pleasant. The rain water had drained off the field, leaving firm ground. The crowds came early and in large numbers. They arrived by lake boat, by stage, by wagons, by buggies, on horse back and those nearby walked to the grounds. There was a good show and a fine variety of displays. There was a keen competition in the cattle and animal section.

The crowds enjoyed the outing. It is estimated some 7,000 visitors attended the show. The Annual Dinner of the Association, held in the dining hall of the Market Square was a feature. On the Friday afternoon, a ploughing match, a steeple chase and a rifle shoot provided added attractions. The prize winning displays were of a high quality, and a large number of Cobourg people were winners in various categories. The Indians of Alderville and of Rice Lake gained special mention for their craft work displays.

Newspapers gave the Exhibition good coverage with feature writeups in the American Buffalo papers. The fair was a big success. It set the Annual Provincial Exhibition on a sound basis for many years of successful, progressive shows. The Association returned to Cobourg for the second time in the year 1855. That fair, too, was held at the same site as the 1848 show. Ultimately the Provincial phased out and the Canadian National Exhibition served in its place.

Local Improvements in Cobourg

The President and Board of Police form of local government looked after the affairs and the business of the Corporation from 1837 through the year 1849. During this period, a number of interested and capable men sat on the Board. They served the town without any personal financial remuneration. In fact, at times, they furnished their own money as a loan to the town in times of need and short supply of specie.

Cobourg grew and prospered. On two or three occasions the Cobourg Act of Incorporation was amended to provide some special or added powers for the Board of Police. One alteration was made in 1846. Special power was given for the installation of common sewers or storm drains in the town streets, and assess the cost of the same against the properties abutting such work. In the fall of 1847, a brick, arched-shaped, storm-water sewer was installed under King Street from the small creek, westward to Ontario Street. This was Cobourg's first permanent sewer and it continues to give service to this day.

In the year 1922, the writer was employed as the field engineer's assistant on the initial paving work in King Street. Underground services of various kinds were installed or restored, preliminary to the laying down of the pavement. Catch basin connections for storm water outlets were made to this old brick sewer, which was found to be in a sound condition at that time. During the course of that summer, the writer had a good view of the underside of King Street, observing its soils and appurtenances.

At one time in 1848, when circulating specie was in short supply, the Board of Police issued "shin-plasters", for local circulation between town employees, contractors, merchants and tax paying persons. An editorial of March, 1848 boosts this idea.

In 1847, the President and Board of Police purchased a house and lot situated at the corner of Third and King Streets, adjacent to the town owned property. Later in 1853, the Town Council purchased an additional strip on Third Street, behind the 1847 purchase, thus making the Market Square continuous between Second and Third Streets. Sometimes the best of plans can be flawed. In the year of 1863, it came to light and to be known that a widow had a claim to the land then occupied by the new Victoria Hall and the Market Square. Someone had failed to provide for her dower rights in a very early land transaction. As a result she collected a handsome sum from the town, and since that time the Town-Hall Market-Square property has enjoyed a clear title.

Responsible Government

One of the prime purposes of this history is to give in detail the various developments in Local Government up to and including the arrival of Responsible Government in the year 1850.

From the time of Lieutenant Governor John Graves Simcoe, the power in local government came from the top down through the appointed Executive Council, the District Magistrates, also appointees, meeting in their Quarter Seasions, who in turn took over where Town Meetings failed to function. The Town officials appointed at Town Meetings were responsible to the Magistrates.

The Ministry of Robert Baldwin and Louis Lafontaine reformed the system of

Municipal Government. This change replaced the Board of Police in towns like Cobourg, and established the Town Council and Mayor group. Cobourg had gained, in a sense, responsible government at the time of its incorporation in

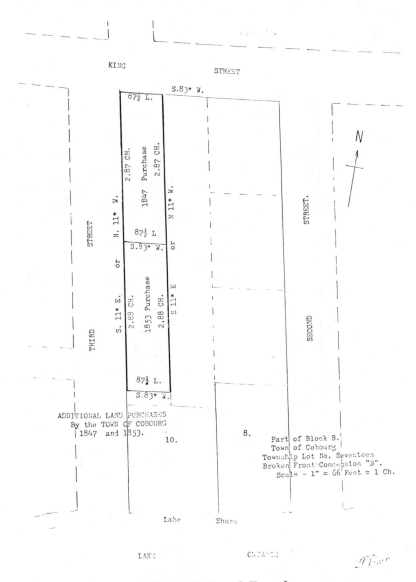

**Additional Land Purchases
By the Town of Cobourg
1847 and 1853**

Release of Dower Settlement
1863
by the Town of Cobourg

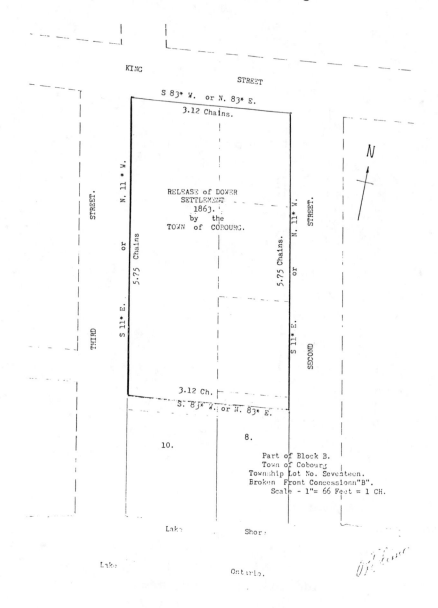

1837. The new Act eliminated the Annual Town Meeting and gave the Townships an elected Council. It changed the make-up of the District Councils to the new arrangement of County Councils. It brought in provisions for an incorporated Village with an elective Council. With the new Act, Power came from below, from the "grass Roots", through the voter, upwards. The elective groups were made responsible to the voters who placed them in office.

The following is a partial outline of the new Act and the local government changes that came into effect on January 1st, 1850. Responsible Government in local affairs had finally arrived.

New Municipal Bill

Townships

It provides that each township shall be an incorporated municipality having five Councillors, to be elected annually, one of which is to be chosen Town-reeve, who presides at meetings, and is a County Councillor. Township municipalities are authorized to make By-Laws for the following purposes: — — The purchase of real property, erection of Town Hall, School Houses, Pounds, appoint Pound keepers, construct and repair drains and water courses, open and improve roads, Etc., regulating driving over bridges, regulation of inns, taverns, etc., grant money for improving roads, restrain animals from running at large, impose tax on dogs, etc., destruction of weeds, sale of animals impounded, settling height of fences, establish boundary lines, compounding of statute labour, enforcing statute labour, impose fines, borrow money, levying moneys, make local regulations, repeal, Etc., by-laws.

Counties

Counties of Upper Canada incorporated: town-reeves of townships, etc., in each county, to constitute Municipal Council of such County. Roads Etc., to be under the jurisdiction of counties through which they run. Councils may make by-laws for the purchase of real property, meeting the expenses of pupils attending the University of Toronto, Etc., whose parents are unable to incur such expenses; endowment of fellowships; Etc., in University; appoint inspectors of House of Industry; remunerate County Officers, prevent immoderate driving on highways, grant licenses to Road and Bridge Companies, Etc.

Police Villages

Police regulations to be enforced with respect to ladders on roofs, buckets; baker's, brewer's and ashery chimneys, (to be three feet higher than buildings within one chain); stove-pipes, entering certain places with candles, Etc., lighting fires in wooden houses etc.,: vessels for conveying fire; hay, straw, Etc., (not to be kept in any dwelling); keeping and sale of gun powder; (in metal in all cases, and not to be sold by candlelight) deposit of ashes— — must not be in wooden vessels; Quick lime not to be left near wood; lighting fires in streets —

five shillings fine; charcoal furnaces for making charcoal forbidden within limits; filth, rubbish Etc., fineable if thrown into streets, or left there.

Incorporated Villages

Village municipalities may make by-laws for opening new roads and streets, or selling old roads or streets; remove steps; regulate markets; regulate harbours; assize of bread; enforce observation of the Sabbath; lock-up houses; public cemeteries; immoderate driving; injuring trees.

Towns

Inhabitants of towns mentioned in schedule B and C incorporated. (Cobourg included.)

Three Councillors to be chosen for every ward. Election — — first Monday in January. Qualifications for Councillor — 500 Pounds real property assessed. Electors — male freeholders, and proprietors or tennants assessed at 25 Pounds. A Police office in each town; Police Magistrate, to be a barrister of three years' standing; salary not less than 100 Pounds; not to be appointed until petitioned for by the Corporation; three assessors and one collector for each ward. — — Town Council to consist of Councillors from each ward. Powers granted to Town Councils to make by-laws for — — establishing Police almhouses etc., Purchases of land for industrial farm; lighting with gas, oil etc.; Livery stable licenses, (regulate their charges.); assess real property for improvements in the neighbourhood, sweep and water streets; borrow monies.

— — — The Cobourg Star, February 21, 1849

COUNTY DIVISION SUBSTITUTION BILL.
UPPER CANADA. SYNOPSIS

A. Title — Preamble and commencement of Act 1st Jan. 1850.

B. Enactments.

1. Abolition of District Divisions.

Section 2. — District Divisions abolished.

3. District Courts and other District Institutions to be henceforth County Institutions, and all laws applicable to the one to be applied .to the other.

4. Courts of Assize and Nisi Prius, Etc. to be held for Counties as now held for Districts.

11. Union of Counties for municipal, judicial and other purposes.

5. Counties in Schedule A. united for judicial, municipal and all other purposes, except Representation and Registration of Titles, and to have Courts and other Institutions in common while Union continues.

6. Property of United Counties to be held in common. Etc. Etc.

111. Disolution of Unions of Counties. Etc. Etc.

1. Miscellaneous and Temporary Provisions.

26. Public Property of Districts transferred to Counties and Unions of Counties as in Schedule b.

28. Justices of the Peace, Etc. now in office for District, to exercise their functions in Counties and Unions of Counties, as in Schedule B. Etc. Etc.

Schedule A.

8. Northumberland and Durham.

Schedule B.

11. To Northumberland and Durham — — those of the Newcastle District.
— — — The Cobourg Star, March 14, 1849.

The First Cobourg Council

It is unfortunate the issues of the Cobourg newspapers of 1850 are now missing, and we cannot record the editorial comments made at that time of change in the municipal systems.

A new nine-man Council was elected in place of the former fiveman Board. The following was the elected personnel of Cobourg's first Town Council:

ASA A. BURNHAM; FRANCIS BURNET; JAMES CANAVAN; JOHN HELM, Sr.; A. MILNE; GEORGE PERRY; THOMAS SCOTT; R.H. THROOP; and WILLIAM WELLER who was appointed Mayor by his Council, the first Mayor of Cobourg.

One Act of the 1850 Town Council of Cobourg, was to take over and to come into possession of the Cobourg Harbour — but at a price!

The details of this important purchase, the demise of the former Cobourg Harbour Company, and the dealings with the Company Stock holders are all spelled out in "AN ACT to VEST the HARBOUR AT COBOURG in the MUNICIPALITY of THAT TOWN", passed by the Government on the 10th day of August, 1850. For the readers interest, we give the Act here in its complete form:

An Act to Vest the Harbour at Cobourg in the Municipality of that Town — 10 August, 1850

WHEREAS the Harbour at Cobourg has never been completed, notwithstanding that the time allowed to the President Directors and Company of the Cobourg Harbour, for that purpose, has long since expired; And whereas by a certain Indenture, bearing date the eighteenth day of August, One Thousand Eight Hundred and Forty-two, and executed by and between the President, Directors and Company, of the Cobourg Harbour, of the one part, and the Board of Works, of the other part, the said Harbour and its appurtenances were conveyed and assigned to the Board of Works, in security for all such moneys as the Provincial Government in this Province has expended or should expend upon the said Harbour; And WHEREAS the sum of Ten Thousand, Five Hundred Pounds or there about has been expended by the Provincial Government upon and in improving the said Harbour, and for the money so expended, Her Majesty holds the said Harbour, its tolls and appurtenances in security, under and by virtue of the said conveyance of the Board of Works; And WHEREAS the Town Council of the Town of Cobourg have contracted with the Government for the purchase by the Town, of the interest of the Government in the said Harbour and its appurtenances. And it hath been agreed by the Government to assign such interest and the right and title of Her Majesty to the said Harbour and its appurtenances to the Municipal Corporation of the said Town for a consideration agreed upon; And WHEREAS in consequence of the non-completion of the said Harbour, and its present imperfect state, the stock of the said Company has become very much depreciated in value; And WHEREAS the Town Council of the Town of Cobourg have agreed with divers of the Stock Holders of the said Company for the purchase of the Stock held by them and are desirous of becoming possessed of the said Harbour, and of having the management and control thereof; And WHEREAS it is most desirable that the said Harbour should be rendered and made safe commodious and convenient as possible, and the said Town Council are interested on behalf of the said Town of Cobourg in improving and keeping improved the said Harbour for the purpose of trade of the said Town, and attracting hither vessels navigating the Lake; And Whereas the said Company have, by non-completion of the said Harbour within the time prescribed by their Act of Incorporation, and the Acts amending the same, rendered themselves liable to the forfeiture of the rights, privileges, and powers conferred upon them as such a Company, and to have their Act of Incorporation declared void; BE IT THEREFORE ENACTED by the Queen's Most Excellent Majesty, by and with the advice and consent of the Legislative Council and of the Legislative Assembly of the Province of Canada constituted and assembled by virtue of and under the authority of an Act passed in the Parliament of the United Kingdom of Great Britain and Ireland, and entituled, An Act to re-unite the Provinces of Upper and Lower Canada, and for the Government of Canada, and it is hereby enacted by the Authority of the same, that the Corporation of the President, Directors and Company of the Cobourg Harbour, created by the Act of the Parliament of Upper Canada, passed in the tenth year of the Reign of King George the Fourth, and entituled An Act to Improve the Navigation of Lake Ontario by Authorizing the Construction of a Harbour at Cobourg, by a Joint Stock Company, shall be, and the said Corporation is hereby dissolved; And the said Act, and Acts amending it shall cease from and after the passing of this Act, so far as regards anything to be done by the said Corporation or the Stockholders thereof, subject nevertheless to the provisions hereinafter contained in favour of those now holding stock in the said Company; And the Assignment made by the Provincial Government to the Municipal Corporation of the said Town is hereby confirmed and made valid, and the sum thereby agreed to be paid by the said Corporation shall be a debt due to Her Majesty by it.

II.

And be it enacted, that the said Harbour and all land attached thereto, and the moles, piers, wharves, buildings, erections and appurtenances, and all other things now erected, or being or belonging to or used with or in the said Harbour and heretofore vested in the said Company, and all other moles, piers, wharves, buildings and erections to be hereafter erected, set up or established in the said Harbour, and all materials which shall be from time to time, got or provided for constructing, building, repairing or maintaining the said Harbour or the erections therein made, or the appurtenances thereto, and all claims for sums of money due to the said Company for tolls, and all tolls which the said Town Council are by this Act authorized to levy, and all rents, issues, profits, fees, emoluments derivable or to be derived from the said Harbour, and appurtenances and everything thereto belonging shall be and the same are hereby vested in the Municipal Corporation of the Town of Cobourg for ever, and shall be under the control and management, and within the jurisdiction of the Council of the said Town; and the said Harbour in its present or future state; and with any additions that may be made thereto, shall and the same is hereby declared to be within the limits and be part of the said Town of Cobourg; and all sums of money due to the said Company for tolls may be sued for and recovered by the said Municipal Corporation by virtue of this Act. PROVIDED always that when recovered, all such sums shall be the property of the Company for the benefit of such Stock Holders as in the sixth section mentioned; and whenever such sums shall amount to a sum sufficient to pay a dividen of three percent to such stockholders, such dividend shall be declared at such rate percent as shall cover the balance remaining unpaid.

III

And be it enacted, that the said Town Council shall and may have power and they are hereby authorized by By-Laws, subject to the approval of the Governor in Council, to fix and determine and to alter from time to time as they may see fit, the rate of tolls to be chargeable and paid on all vessels and boats entering the said Harbour, and on all goods, chattels, wares and merchandise shipped or landed on board, or out of any vessel or boat in the said Harbour, or between the eastern boundary of Lot Number Thirteen, and the western boundary of Lot Number Twenty-one, in the Township of Hamilton, in the County of Northumberland, and to ask, demand and recover and receive the same to and for the use of the said Town Council; and in case of neglect or refusal by any person or persons owning or in charge of any vessel, boat, goods, chattels, wares, merchandise, to pay the tolls legally collectable thereon under the Act, or in case of any vessel, boat, goods, chattels, wares or merchandise, on which such tolls may be chargeable, lying or remaining in or adjacent, adjunct to such Harbour, unclaimed and without the tolls thereon being paid for ten days after such toll shall have been legally chargeable thereon, to seize and detain the vessels, boats, goods, chattels, wares and merchandise on which such tolls may be due, payable or chargeable, and if such tolls shall remain unapid thereon for the space of twenty days after such seizure, then to sell and dispose of such goods, chattels, wares, merchandise, vessels or boats, by and at public auction, for the best price than can be obtained for the same, first giving ten days notice thereof by inserting the same in the newspaper (if any) published in the Town of Cobourg, and by putting up a notice on some conspicuous place in the said Harbour, and out of the proceeds of such sale, to deduct and pay the tolls in arrears and unpaid upon the things sold; and the expenses of and incident to such sale, and the residue, if any, to pay over when demanded to the owner or owners of the things so sold.

IV.

AND be it enacted, that it shall and may be lawful for the said Town Council, and they are hereby empowered to make such additions and improvements in and to the said Harbour, as they from time to time may think fit; and to make and adopt from time to time such By-Laws and Regulations and enter into such contracts as they shall approve, for managing and controlling the said Harbour, and leasing any portion or portions thereof, and improving or adding to the said Harbour, and to employ such servants and agents in and about the business of the said Harbour as they shall require, and generally to do and perform all such Acts and exercise all such powers as shall be necessary for the efficient management of the said Harbour, and the contract for purchase and take conveyances of and to and for the purpose of the said Harbour, in extending or improving the same as they may think fit, such additional land as they may acquire, and the same when so acquired, shall vest in the Municipal Corporation of the said Town for ever; and the said Town Council shall and may from time to time, as they shall see fit, sell, depart with and convey any portion of the land now forming part of or attached to, or hereafter to be acquired for or attached to the said Harbour, which they may find unnecessary for the purposes of such Harbour; and in case the said Town Council shall not be able to agree with the owner or owners for any property which they may desire either to purchase absolutely for the use of and purposes of the said Harbour, or in or about which they may desire to make any road, street, cut, drain, or other improvement may be made, shall be reasonably entitled to, such land may be taken and such road, street, cut, drain or other improvements made by the said Council in the manner and subject to the provisions made in and by the one hundred and ninety-fifth; one hundred and ninety-sixth; one hundred and ninety-seventh Sections of the Act passed in the twelth year of Her Majesty's Reign, and intituled, An Act to provide by one general law, for the erection of Municipal Corporation, and the establishment of Regulations of Police in and for the several Counties, Cities, Towns, Township and Villages in Upper Canada which shall apply as if the said Council had been authorized by the said Act to take such land, or to do such thing as aforesaid without the consent of the owner of the property taken or affected.

V.

And be it enacted, that for the purpose of completing and improving the said Harbour, and of erecting additional wharves, moles and piers therein; and of making such other additions and improvements therein as the said Town Council shall resolve on and approve, it shall and may be lawful for the said Town Council, and they are here-by authorized to borrow such sum or sums of money from time to time as they may deem requisite, and if they shall see fit, to secure and provide for payment of the same, by issuing from time to time in the name of the Municipal Corporation of the said Town, debentures for sums not less than one hundred pounds and redeemable within twenty years after the issue thereof with interest at the rate not exceeding eight per cent, per annum, and such debentures shall be transferrable, and the holder or holders of such of them as are not paid withing or at the time at which they shall be made redeemable shall and may sue for and recover against the said Municipal Corporation of the said Town of Cobourg the amount thereof, with the interest thereby agreed to be paid; Provided nevertheless that all such debentures shall, on the face thereof, in some sufficient form of words, show and express that they are issued for or on account of the said Harbour.

VI.

And be it enacted, That all parties who at the time of the passing of this Act, hold any Stock of the Company herein before mentioned, and shall not have sold or tansferred the same to the Municipal Corporation of the said Town, shall be entitled to be, and shall be interested in and considered to hold Stock in the said Harbour to the amount paid up on the stock held by them afforesaid, but without any right nevertheless to interfere in the management or control of the said Harbour; PROVIDED that within six months after the passing of this Act, they notify the said Town Council by writing under their hands respectively the amount of Stock of the said Company held by them at the time of the passing of this Act, and the amount paid up by them on such stock; and the value and the extent of the interest of such persons in the said Harbour shall be regulated in manner following, that is to say: They shall be entitled annually hereafter to a dividend upon the said Stock of the rents, issues, profits, annual fees, and tolls derived from the said Harbour, (After paying all the current expenses and managing the said Harbour, and the interest on any money which may be borrowed from time to time to improve the same, and the interest of the sum expended by the Government upon the said Harbour and now assigned to the Municipal Corporation of the said Town Council) in the proportion which the amount of stock held by them in the said Harbour, shall bear to the aggregate amount assigned by the Government to the Municipal Corporation of the said Town, the sum paid by the said Council to individual stock holders or otherwise in acquiring the said harbour and the sum expended by the said Town in improving and completing the said Harbour; AND so long as any stockholder shall remain, the said Town Council shall Annually, that is to say, on the second Monday in January in each and every year hereafter, publish by insertion thereof in one newspaper, if any published in the Town of Cobourg, and by filing a copy thereof under the Seal of the Corporation, and the hand of the Mayor or Chief Municipal Officer of the Town of Cobourg, in the Office of the Clerk of the Peace for the County in which the said Town is situate, such a statement of the said Harbour and the affairs thereof, as will enable a calculation to be made of the dividend payable according to the Act, to any person or persons holding Stock in the said Harbour, and any person shall be entitled to examine such statement, or make a copy thereof, on paying to the Clerk of the Peace a fee of one shilling and three pence; and the said Town Council shall, on and after the second Monday in January in each and every year, pay the person or persons entitled thereto the dividend or dividends to which he or they may so be entitled, and in default of such payment, such dividends may be sued for and recovered in like manner as other debts due by the said Corporation.

VII.

AND be it enacted, That the Stock held by individuals in the said Harbour under this Act, may be transferred to the said Town Council, or, from time to time, to any person or persons desirous of obtaining the same; Provided that such transfer, unless made to the said Town Council, shall not be binding, or effectual until a memorandum of the same shall have been signed by the transferer and transferee, or their duly authorized attorneys, in such Book of the said Town Council as by the said Town Council may be provided or assigned for that purpose; Provided always, that it shall be lawful during one year from the passing of this Act, for any holder of Stock in the said Harbour to tender the same to the said Municipal Corporation, without projudice to the right of such Sotckholder to receive his dividends as in the proviso to the second section mentioned, and to require the said Corporation to purchase the same at the rate of Sixty-Six Pounds, Thirteen Shillings and Four Pence for every One Hundred pounds of nominal amount of such shares, payable in debentures to be issued by the said Corporation in favor of such shareholder, one third of the principal of such debentures being payable in five years, one third in ten years, and one third in fifteen years from the date of such tender, with interest from the said date payable half yearly; and if the said Corporation shall refuse or neglect to purchase such stock or to issue such debentures, such stock holder shall have the like remedy against them in law or in equity as if they had contracted to purchase such stock from him on the terms aforesaid.

VIII.

And be it enacted, That this Act shall not in any way abridge or be construed to abridge the powers, which, independently of the special provisions therein contained, the said Town Council might or could, may or can, exercise over property within their control or jurisdiction, except when such powers may be inconsistant with this Act.

IX.

AND be it enacted, that this Act shall be a Public Act.

1850 Cobourg Who's Who

Cobourg Seventy-Five Years Ago

(From the Cobourg World, Thursday, March 18, 1926.)

Seventy-five years ago, what had formerly been the village of Cobourg, had been incorporated a short time before as a town, and was presided over by the first Mayor, Wm. Weller, and a council composed of A.A. Burnham, D.E. Boulton, John Beatty, Thomas Eyre, J.A. Gilchrest, A. Jeffrey, Geo. Perry, R.H. Throop. (Note added— The town was incorporated in 1837).

An old resident has presented the World with a list of business men of the town at that time. They were as follows; according to the copy given to us: HENRY ALLEN, Dry goods; WILLIAM ALEXANDER, Saloon; JAMES H. ARMSTRONG, shoemaker; JAMES AUSTIN, M.D.; J. BAIN, printer; MISS BATE, milliner; JOSEPH BATES, grocer; DR. BEATTY, M.D.; Rev. JOHN BEATTY, Wesleyan minister; JOHN BEATTY, grocer; BURTON BENNETT, barrister at law; Rev. Dr. BETHUNE, Church of England minister; J.N. BOSWELL, chemist and druggist; D.E. BOULTON, Barrister at Law; ROBERT BUDGE, tailor; W. and D. BURNET, carpenters, etc.; JOHN BUTLER, grocer; LEWIS BRANGEL, cooper; Rev. JOHN BREDIN, Wesleyan minister; JAMES CALCUTT, Jr., dry goods; JAMES CALCUTT, brewer; F.G. CALLENDER, dentist; JAMES CANAVAN, carpenter; JAMES CHITTICK, smith and farrier; BENJAMIN CLARK, general store; THOMAS B. CLENCH, cabinet maker; JAMES COCKBURN, Barrister at Law; SAMUEL COLLINS, blacksmith; JAMES CUTHBERT, shoe store; JAMES DROPE, grocer; JOS. DUBEAN, tailor and clothier; W. DUMBLE, clothier; H. DUNCAN, farrier; Rev. H. Elliott, Bible Christian Minister; J. FLETCHER, shoemaker; ARCHIBALD FRASER, tailor; FIELD & BRO., general store; JOHN GEE, innkeeper; THOMAS GILLBARD, tailor; WM. GILLBARD, grocer; JAMES GILCHRIST, medical doctor: JAMES GORDON, grocer; WM. GRIEVES, joiner and builder; JOHN GUILLET, grocer; ANDREW HALLIDAY, saddler; THOMAS HOLLOWELL, M.D.; P. HANCOCK, boatmaker; THOMAS HARVEY, general store; ANTHONY HAWKEY, saddler; M.F. HOBART, cabinet maker; JOHN HOOEY, baker; JAMES HOSSACK, bookstore; —?— HORTON, leather store; STUART HOOEY, grocer; FRNKLIN HOUSE, bookseller; J.F. HURST, hardware; SAMUEL IRWIN, cooper; ANDREW JEFFREY, hardware; Rev. H.B. JESSUPP, Church of England Minister; THOMAS JEWELL, grocer; THOMAS JUDGE, boot maker; THOMAS KERSHAW, general smith; PATRICK KEWIN, baker; A.S. KENNEDY, boots and shoes; WM. KNOWLES, stone cutter; REV. S.W. LADU, Episcopal Methodist Minister; WM. LAURIE, innkeeper, SYLVESTER LEWIS, marble factory; JNO. LOCKHEAD, grocer,

PETER McCALLUM, tailor and merchant; ARCHIBALD McDONALD, barrister-at-law; JAMES McGRAN, innkeeper; MICHAEL McKENNEY, grocer; Rev. Donald McLEOD, Free Church Minister,; ARTHUR MacBEAN, general store; RICHARD MEANS, cabinet maker; JOHN MITCHELL, grocer; J.W. THOMPSON, operator Montreal Telegraph Company; THOMAS MORROW, saddler; MATTHEW MORROW, baker; ANDREW MOSCREPT, foundry; A.C. MUNSON, carriage maker; NEWS ROOM, King Street; Rev. S. NELLES, Wesleyan Minister, GEORGE NIXON, chandler; JOHN NOBLE, bootmaker; WM. PAYNE, grocer; CHARLES POMEROY, carpenter; POMEROY BROS., general store; C. POOL, surgeon dentist; Mrs. W.F. POWELL, milliner; THOMAS PRATT, baker; ALEXANDER PRINGLE, watchmaker; PATRICK REGAN, livery stables; SAMUEL RICHARDSON, cooper; Rev. PAUL ROBINS, Bible Christian Minister; JOHN ROBERTS, shoes; JOHN RUSSELL, bootmaker; RICHARD RUTTAN, Barrister-at-law; THOMAS SALISBURY, innkeeper; A. SECORD, hatter and furrier; WM. SMITH, innkeeper; SIDNEY SMITH, barrister; JOHN SMITH, innkeeper; Rev. I. SNELL, Congregational Minister; P. SNOW, tailor; GEORGE STePHENS, cabinet maker; ALEXANDER STEWART, carpenter; JOHN SUTHERLAND, grocer; Rev. L. TAYLOR, Wesleyan Minister; HENRY TERRY, general store; GEORGE THOMPSON, shoemaker; ROBERT THROOPE, barriater-at-law; Rev. MICHAEL TIMLIN, Roman Catholic Priest; Rev. C. VANDUSEN, Wesleyan Minister; GEORGE VOSPER, Carpenter and builder; JAMES WILSON, innkeeper.

All the prominent men of the town and of those taking part in its municipal life, are not mentioned in this record, for other records show that Mr. Thomas Scott was then Post Master. William Weller had charge of the Royal Mail Line of stage coaches running between Toronto and Montreal. Thomas Eyre and George M. Goodeve were auditors of the town; Robert Craig was Chief Constable and surveyor of streets; David Brodie was clerk and treasurer, and there were probably a number of others.

Tidal Wave at Cobourg

The tidal wave which extended along Lake Ontario for about twenty-four or twenty-five miles early Saturday morning, including Cobourg within its range, affected the water in the harbour here to a very noticeable extent. Ontario No. One was in the harbour, and the water is stated to have raised about four feet, elevating boat and deck and then receded to such an extreme that it was reported the big steamer was almost left stranded. However it is probable that it was only the sudden inflow of water into the harbour passing out again. The cause of the strange occurrence, which was a very unusual one for this port, is apparently a mystery. At Rochester and other ports along the south shore the tidal wave swept quite a distance inland and considerable damage was done.

— The Cobourg World, May 28, 1925.

Note; It is on record, and reported in the Cobourg Star, September 24, 1845, that a similar tidal wave was noted at the Cobourg Harbour and at other places along the lake. The explanation is given is a later edition of the Star, November 26, 1845. The tidal wave was produced by an extreme differential in barometric pressure over an area of the lake.

With the presentation of this history of Cobourg into the year 1850, the writer hopes some former false impressions, incorrect statements and other errors that have made for some misunderstandings will be better understood and made more clear. We all can err, but prime sources have been used throughout this work. The above published list of first Councillors for Cobourg is a sample of errors. August 16, 1984.

A Closing Story
The Queen and The Old Swimming Hole

My wife, Betty, and I had received an invitation to visit Cobourg to see the Queen. We drove from St. Catharines arriving in good time to park our car on Burnham Street. We walked the full length of Heath Street to the footpath entrance into the Honorable James Cockburn Park. The day was beautiful with warm summer breezes, and lazy clouds allowing the sun to shine through. It was a perfect day for the Queen to visit Cobourg.

On crossing William Street, a very fine sight met our eyes. Spread before us was the panorama of acres of fresh, green-grass park, sloping gently down to the Factory Creek. A new steel footbridge spanned the stream. Beyond, more areas of greenery, plus a grove of cedars, caught our vision. The southerly hillside beyond the creek was almost hid behind tall willows. Here two branches of the Factory Creek joined immediately downstream from the footbridge. Above the bridge a small dam held back a pond. It was a beautiful sight.

Crowds had already gathered. We walked down the roped-off pathway, across the footbridge, and took our seats reserved for special guests. The recently erected cairn had a Royal Purple cover over its plaque. A canopy-covered platform had been placed some fifty feet in front of the cairn. Two young maple trees, one on each side of the cairn, were in readiness for the Royal planting.

Soon many more people arrived. Colour parties took their places. Dignitaries came and were seated... School children carrying hand flags, scout troups, girl guides and brownies, militia personnel, bands in uniform, police, veterans decorated with medals, photographers, senior citizens, and many others came. All contributed colour and movement to the scene.

As we sat waiting the arrival of the Queen and her party, our thoughts reviewed the various historical events and places in this corner of old Cobourg, freshly brought to memory by the souvenir edition of the Cobourg Star newspaper. Here we were, deep in the Honorable James Cockburn Park, officially named in

Centennial Year of Canada's Confederation. To the north-west, the Golden Plough Lodge marks the site of the ancient Newcastle District capital and the former village of Amherst. In the same Direction, the modern United Counties building borders the park. Old names like Asa and Zaccheus Burnham, Sheriff Ruttan, William Weller, Sidney Smith, James Cockburn and others come to mind. Cobourg has had a very interesting historical past.

The new fresh, green park, with neatly trimmed lawns; the new steel bridge; the small new dam; the placid pond; and the gathering crowds fade out of one's physical vision. The mind's eye takes over, and the memory bank of some fifty-five years previous brings to the fore old scenes of my boyhood.

There comes to view an ancient pasture field filled with rank and high grass and tall weeds. An old wire fence borders William Street. Clumps of cedar and willow grow in the area betwwen the street and the creek. A dense cedar grove was to the north-east. Tall willows screened the hillside across the creek. Downstream, one quarter of a mile distant, an old mill-dam held back the creek water. An ancient, A-frame truss, single-span, wooden bridge spanned the mill-pond on William Street. The quiet water backed up the two streams, giving depth at their junction. Here was the "old swimming hole". My father bathed here in his boyhood, back in the 1860's. Here, generation after generation of Cobourg boys learned how to swim. It was traditional to take the first dip of the season at this spot on the 24th of May, when Canada celebrated the old Queen's birthday. This was a very favourite place for Cobourg boys to enjoy the freshness of clean stream water. This is an historic spot, very dear to many old Cobourg boys, many that have long since passed on.

The old dam disappeared. The old wooden bridge is but a faint memory. The old pond is now a running brook. The deeper pool has been replaced with shallow water. A new steel foot-bridge spans the site of the old swimming hole.

On Wednesday, June 27, 1973, Her Royal Majesty, the radiant Queen Elizabeth II, accompanied by Mr. Edwin R. Haynes of Cobourg, followed by her husband, Prince Philip and Mrs. Haynes and other dignitaries, walked down the new path from William Street and crossed over the new steel bridge. In doing so, the Royal Couple passed over the "old swimming hole", a place of fond memory to many an old Cobourg boy.

*Victor W. Climo enjoying a "skinny dip" in the "old swimming hole"
— June 30th, 1913.*

*Her Britannic Majesty, Queen Elizabeth II, Queen of Canada, walks over the site of
the "old swimming hole" accompanied by Mr. E.R. Haynes of Cobourg on Wednesday
June 27th, 1973.*

A Song of a Young Lad

When Pa was a little boy like me
He used to go in swimmin', in swimmin', in swimmin'.
He used to go 'way up the creek
Where there was no fear of wimmin, of wimmin, of wimmin.
One day
Some people happened to pass that way
And stole dear Pa's apparel, apparel, apparel.
My Pa swam around in the water all day
And at night went home in a barrel, in a barrel, in a barrel.
POOR PA!

A History of Cobourg into the year 1850

References

The Saga of the Great Lakes, re-published by the Coles Publishing Company limited, 1980. Reprinted from the famous History of the Great Lakes, originally published by J.H. Beers & Co. in 1899.

The Cobourg World newspaper, June and July, 1914.
Personal observations.
Canada — An Outline of History — J.A. Lower — Ryerson Press.
Indian Treaties — Counties of Northumberland and Durham. — The Dept. of Indian Affairs.

Instructions to Mr. Augustus Jones, D.P.S. from J. Collins, Esq. Deputy Surveyor General.

Field Notes of Augustus Jones.
"John Graves Simcoe, Lieutenant Governor of Upper Canada."
"The Positive side of John Graves Simcoe." by Mattie M.I. Clark.
Association of Ontario Land Surveyors. — 1924 Report re AARON GREELEY.
The Russell Papers — Vol. III — Page 257.
Sessions of the Second Parliament of Upper Canada.
The Valley of the Trent — By E.C. Guilett.
COBOURG — 1798—1948.

Land Settlement in Upper Canada — 16th Report-Dept of Archives, 1920 by Alexander Fraser.

Archives of Ontario records — Census lists for Hamilton Township.
Assessment Rolls for Hamilton Township.
The COBOURG STAR newspaper — 1831—1849.
The Kingston Chronicle newspaper April of 1819.
The Cobourg Sentinel newspaper March 1874.
The Cobourg Registry Office — Old Deeds.
etc.
Historical Reminiscences of Cobourg — By Daniel McAllister — 1903.
Victorian Cobourg — 1976 — Mica Publishing Company.
Various issues of the Cobourg World Newspaper.

INDEX

Index to Place Names, et cetera
(Surnames listed separately)

A

Act of Incorporation, 82
Albany, 102
Albion Hotel, 92, 130
Alderville, 133
Alnwick Twp., 6
American Colonies, 6, 7, 37
American Revolution, 4, 24
Amherst; Village of, 41, 42, 47, 50, 60, 61, 62, 63, 66, 67, 71, 88, 124
Anglican Church, 70
Annual Town Meeting, 66, 88, 105, 137
Archives of Ontario, 7, 11, 61, 123
Assessors, 39
Asiatic Cholera, 64
Atlantic, 63, 64

B

Bay of Quinte, 4, 6, 8, 11, 13, 14, 23, 25, 43, 47
Bath, Village of, 60, 102, 125
Battell's Inn, 81, 82
Belleville, 25, 60, 66, 102
Bible Christians, 99
Board of Health, 64
Board of Police, 63, 72, 74, 75, 80, 81, 82, 83, 86, 87, 88, 89, 90, 94, 97, 99, 101, 102, 105, 113, 114, 116, 125, 129, 133, 134, 135.
Board of Trade, 90, 92, 119
Board of Works, 123, 124, 139, 140
Brighton, 102
British North America, 4
British Parliament, 4

British Throne, 1
Brockville, 47, 60
Brown's Inn, 81, 82
Buckville, 51, 52

C

Canada, 4
Canada Act, 4, 5
Canada's Confederation, 1
Canada Day, 4
Cape Cod, 19
Carrying Place, 4, 60
Cataraqui, 24
Chippawa, 94
Church of England, 6, 47, 65, 70, 90, 98, 108
Chicago, 14
Church of Scotland, 70
Circuit Riders, 45
Clarke; Twp. of, 7, 35, 42, 102
Clergy Reserves, 68, 70
Cobourg's Act of Incorporation, 72 to 81 inclusive
Cobourg 1798-1948, 18
Cobourg Elective Police Bill, 67
Cobourg Incorporation Bill, 71
Cobourg Brook, 124
Cobourg and District Historical Society, 58
Cobourg and Amherst Fire Company, 61
Cobourg Fire Company, 67
Cobourg Harbour Co., 58, 67, 80, 111, 112, 122, 123, 124, 139
Cobourg Historical Society, 24, 25, 28
Cobourg Horse Show, 2
Cobourg Hotel, 59

Cobourg Railway Co., 67, 68, 69, 122
Cobourg Rectory, 70
Cobourg Registry Office, 21, 123
Cobourg Rifles, 93, 94
Cobourg Sentinel, 151
Cobourg Sentinel-Star, 17, 18
Cobourg Star, 18, 41, 59, 65, 67, 68, 71,
81, 82, 83, 87, 88, 89, 90, 92, 97, 99, 100,
101, 103, 104, 105, 106, 107, 111, 119, 120,
121, 124, 125, 126, 129, 131, 138, 139, 147,
151
Cobourg Steam-Boat Company, 123
Cobourg World, 5, 17, 22, 25, 26, 28, 30,
52, 54, 145, 146, 151
Colborne, 57, 60, 102, 132
Colborne District, 105, 106, 111
Colborne Harbour, 25
Collector; The, 39
Commercial Bank, 64, 128
Common School House, 57, 71, 89
County Council, 137
County Town, 2
Court House, 66
Cold Springs, 98
Congregational Church, 98
Cramahe; Twp. of, 8, 9, 11, 12, 15, 23, 29,
34, 35, 43
Crossen Car Shops, 2
Crown Land Records, 24

D
Danbury, Conn., 19
Darlington; Twp. of, 35, 42, 102
Detroit, 102
Detroit River, 6
District Council, 105, 137
District Land Board, 31
District Magistrates, 66, 72, 88, 134
District School House, 52, 60, 61, 66
District Town, 2, 88
Dominion Archives, 111
Dominion Day, 1
Dutch Reformed Church, 47
Dutchy of Cornwall, 99
Durham; County of, 33, 34, 132, 139

E
Elizabethtown, 47
Elsworth's Bridge, 63
England, 6
Etobicoke River, 4
Europe, 64
Executive Council, 30

F
Factory Creek, 21, 56, 121, 124, 133, 147
Family Compact, 69
Fire Companies, 63
Fleming's Map, 116
Forestville, N.Y., 27
Frodingham, Yorkshire, 98
Frontenac Steam Boat, 52

G
Garneau's History of Canada, 6
Gage's Creek, 8
George Ham's Mills, 109
Genesee, 65
Glebe lands, 70
Globe Hotel, 115, 120
Globe Newspaper, 108
Golden Plough Lodge, 41
Governor's Inn, 47
Grafton, 47, 102, 116, 132
Grantham, Twp. of, 21, 24
Great Britain, 48, 57, 64, 72
Great Lakes, 3, 4
Great Migration; the, 63

H
Haldimand; Twp. of, 6, 8, 9, 12, 15, 23,
24, 25, 29, 35, 42, 43
Hamilton, 52, 102, 132
Hamilton; Village of, 52
Hamilton Mills, 111
Hamilton; Twp. of, 1, 5, 6, 8, 9, 11, 12,
15, 19, 21, 25, 27, 30, 31, 34, 35, 38, 41,
42, 43, 47, 48, 50, 54, 57, 66, 88, 122, 124,
151
Ham's Mills, 56
Hardscrabble, 51, 52
Hastings, 5
Home District, 33, 34
Home for the Aged, 2
Hope; Twp. of, 8, 12, 15, 30, 35, 42, 43, 47
Hull's Corners, 47, 50, 52, 54, 66, 88
Humber River, 4

I
Ireland, 64

J
Jones' Creek, 124

K
Kanata, 4
Kelly Hill, 25
King's College, 13

Kingston, 5, 24, 26, 28, 29, 48, 50, 59, 60, 65, 97, 102, 104, 107, 115, 122, 124
Kingston Chronicle, 52, 151

L

Labrador, 3
Lake Iroquois, 3
Lake Ontario, 3, 4, 43, 44, 46, 48, 49, 52, 53, 55, 58, 64, 65, 67, 80, 91, 124, 133, 135, 136, 140, 146
Lakeport, 7
Lennox, 5
Lieutenant Governor, 7
Lindsay, 24
London, 102
Lower Canada, 4, 5, 92, 140
"Loyalists of Ontario", 21

M

Manitoulin Island, 29, 30
MacKechnie's Woolen Mill, 115
Methodists, 45, 47, 50, 52, 57, 60, 65, 66, 70, 98, 99
Methodist Academy, 60
Methodist Chapel, 90
Methodist Church, 54
Methodist Circuit Rider, 54, 56
Militia Day, 60
Mississippi, 3
Monomoit, Mass., 19
Moira River, 25
Mount Moriah Lodge, 47
Montreal, 50, 54, 56, 68, 102, 112, 115, 122, 146
Montreal; Bank of, 128
Murray; Twp. of, 5, 8, 34, 35, 42, 47

N

Napanee, 102
Navy Island, 94, 109
Napoleonic Wars, 48, 50, 57
Newark, 5
Newcastle, District of, 31, 33, 34, 35, 41, 47, 52, 58, 60, 61, 62, 72, 73, 74, 76, 94, 98, 99, 105, 109, 111, 126, 139, 148
Newcastle District Council, 105, 132
Newcastle Turf Club, 110
New England States, 6
New Hampshire, 8, 11, 24
New York, 102
New York State, 11
Niagara, 4, 5, 6, 21, 23, 43, 65, 94, 109

North American Continent, 3
North Star Lodge, 47
Northumberland Agricultural Society, 31, 57, 60, 132
Northumberland; County of, 3, 5, 6, 7, 8, 11, 18, 33, 34, 43, 57, 139
Northumberland Hall, 57
Northumberland Militia, 93
Norwich, England, 19

O

Ohio, 3
Ontario Mills, 48, 110, 114, 126
Ottawa, 111
Ottawa River, 4
Overseer of Highways, 39

P

Park; The Hon. James Cockburn, 147
Path Masters, 66
Percy; Twp. of, 6, 12, 15, 35
Peterborough, 48, 105, 132
Pickering, 102
Police Village, 60, 63, 66, 71, 88
Port Hope, 31, 52, 57, 102, 116, 122, 124
Port Trent, 102
Potash Street, 54
Pound Keepers, 40
Plains of Abraham, 5
Precambrian Shield, 3
Presbyterians, 47, 66, 70, 98, 107
Prescott, 65
Presqu'ile, 24, 41, 98
Province of Canada, 103
Provincial Agricultural Association, 132
Public School, 52

Q

Quarter Sessions, 37, 38, 41, 61, 62, 63, 66, 72, 88, 134
Quebec, 4, 5, 47, 72, 102
Quebec Act, 3
Queen's College, 107
Queenston, 102

R

Regiment; 66th, 93
Regiment; 78th, 6
Registrar, 57
Registry Office, 12
Responsible Government, 137
Rice Lake, 56, 60, 66, 68, 116, 122, 133
Rice Lake Railway, 66

Rochester, 67, 146
Roman Catholic, 99

S

Sandwich, 102
Salmon City, 52
Saxe-Coburg-Gothe, 101
St. Andrew's Church, 107
Scarborough, 102
St. Catharines, 147
Scotch Church, 90
Shannonville, 102
Shelter Valley, 25
Sheriff, 57
"Shin-plasters", 134
Seymour; Twp. of, 6
Sidney; Twp. of, 5, 23
Simcoe; County of, 33
St. John's Lodge, 47
St. Lawrence, 6
Smith's Creek, 4, 43, 47
Smith's Creek Circuit, 56
"Speedy" sailboat, 41
Steamer "Caroline", 94
Steamboat "Cobourg", 64, 65, 98, 111, 113, 122, 123
St. Peter's Church, 51, 66
St. Polycarp Church, 99
Surveyor General, 7

T

"The Church" Newspaper, 24, 108
"The Kirk", 66
"This is Cobourg", 17, 18
"Torbech", 125
Toronto, 19, 65, 93, 94, 97, 102, 108, 109, 111, 113, 114, 115, 122, 123, 132, 146
Toronto Harbour, 23
Town Clerk, 38, 40
Town Meetings, 34, 37
Town of Newcastle, 41
Town Wardens, 40
Township Councils, 38
Treaty of Paris, 4
Trent River, 4, 5

U

Union Jack, 1
United Empire Loyalists, 47, 48
United Kingdom, 51, 63
United Lodge, 47
United States, 7, 11, 47, 50, 51, 64, 98, 103
Union Government, 123

Union Parliament, 104
Upper Canada, 4, 5, 6, 12, 21, 27, 33, 37, 45, 47, 51, 63, 68, 70, 72, 92, 103, 104, 125, 140
Upper Canada Academy, 108
Upper St. Lawrence, 4
Utica, N.Y., 102
"His Settlement of Upper Canada", 24

V

Vermont, 7, 11, 28
Victoria Hall, 54, 97, 134
Victoria Park, 2
Victorian Era, 1, 2

W

Warkworth Journal, 5
Watertown, N.Y., 102
Wallace's Pond, 121
Weller's Coach Factory, 108
West Lake, 25
Whitby, 29, 98, 102
Windsor Bay, 98
Wilder's Inn, 81, 82
White's Mills, 88

Y

Yonge Street, 47
York, 11, 30, 47, 59, 60, 61, 64
York; County of, 33

Index to Surnames
(Placenames et cetera listed separately)

A

Abbes; Nathaniel, 12
Abby; Nathaniel, 34
Alexander; William, 129, 145
Allan; A.G., 93
Allen; Henry, 145
Alley; Moses, 21, 22, 51, 54
Arkwright; Sir Richard, 126
Armour; R., 93
Armour; Shaw, 111
Armstrong, J., 128
Armstrong, James H., 145
Armstrong, Mrs., 129
Ash; George, 12
Ash; George Jr., 12
Ash; James, 12
Ash; Joseph, 12, 34, 58
Ash; Margaret, 43
Ash; Samuel, 12

Austin; James, 145
Auston; ——, 129
Averell; ——, 128

B

Bain; J., 95, 127, 145
Baird; Nicol Hugh, 68
Baldwin; Robert, 134
Bancks (Banks); William, 93
Bate; Miss, 145
Bates; Joseph, 145
Bates; Roger, 48
Bates; Stoddard, 58
Beagan; P., 128
Beamish; J., 115, 128
Beatty; ——, 128
Beatty; J., 128, 129
Beatty; Rev. John, 145
Beatty; Dr., 145
Beatty, John, 145
Beatty; John (grocer), 145
Beatie; W., 115
Bennett; Burton, 145
Bennett; John, 59, 67
Bertram; ——, 121
Bethune; Alexander Neil, 58
Bethune; Rev. Dr., 24, 145
Bethune; Donald, 96
Bethune; James Gray, 50, 51, 56, 58, 59,
63, 64, 110, 122, 125
Bethune; Lieut-Col., 98
Birney; George, 87
Blackstone; Henry, 93
Boswell; G.M., 59, 60, 61, 68
Boswell; G.S., 68
Boswell; J.C., 92
Boswell; J.N., 145
Boswell; J. Vance, 92, 115
Boswell; Hon. Capt. Walter, 58, 68, 92,
105
Boswell; William, 93
Boswell; W.W., 92
Boulter; H., 128
Boulton; D'Arcy E., 99, 101, 111, 129, 145
Boulton; George Strange, 52, 57, 58, 82,
96, 129
Boyder; W., 128
Boyer; George, 115, 120, 128
Boyer; William, 115
Bradbeer; W., 127
Brady; ——, 93
Brangel; Lewis, 145
Bredin; Rev. John, 145
Brewer; ——, 127

Brodie; David, 101, 114, 129, 131, 146
Brodie; J.M., 129
Brook; L.F., 115
Brook; ——, 128
Broughall; L., 127
Brown; Alex, 108
Brown; Richard, 87
Buck; Elijah, 43, 45, 46, 51, 54, 56, 59, 122
Buck; Rowe, 93, 121
Budge; Robert, 128, 145
Buller;; C.G., 93
Burgart; Moses, 12
Burnet; Francis, 101, 139
Burnet; D., 145
Burnet; W., 145
Burnet; Messers, 127
Burnham; Asa, 19, 41, 42, 94, 148
Burnham; Asa A., 71, 129, 139, 145
Burnham; E.E., 41
Burnham; Mark, 47, 56, 125
Burnham; Zaccheus, 8, 63, 148
Burton; F.H., 93
Busby; Ann, 19
Butler; Charles, 93
Butler; John, 129, 145
Butler; William, 93

C

Calcutt; J., 114, 127, 128
Calcutt; James, Sr., 64, 145
Calcutt; Capt., 93, 98
Calcutt; James, 115, 145
Calcutt; W., 130
Callender; G., 128
Callender; F.G., 145
Cameron; ——, 121
Campbell; Dougald, 58, 59, 60, 128
Canavan; J., 127, 139, 145
Canniff; Dr., 24, 25
Carleton; Sir Guy, 6
Carpenter, A.B., 59
Carson; William, 48, 49, 124
Carveth; W., 127
Chaplain; Joseph, 12
Chaplain; Joseph, Jr., 13
Charltain; ——, 127
Chatterton; Richard Dover, 59, 61, 65, 93,
96, 98
Chisholm; Alexander, 34
Chittick; James, 145
Church; L., 60
Church; M., 62
Clark; Benjamin, 115, 120, 128, 145
Clark; Captain, 93

Clarke; C., 64
Clark; J., 127
Clark; Mattie M.I., 151
Clark; Robert, 24
Clench Borthers, 57
Clench; Freeman S., 59, 89, 90, 95, 96, 127
Clench; Thomas B., 145
Cleghorn; T.W., 59
Climo; Percy L., 25
Climo; Victor W., 149
Cockburn; James, 129, 145, 148
Colborne; Sir John, 70
Collins; Mr., 112
Collins, J., 151
Collins; Samuel, 145
Conger; Wilson S., 59, 62, 64, 68, 82, 92, 94, 95, 96, 98, 99, 100, 102, 105, 106
Connell; John, 108
Connelly; J., 129
Corrigal; ——, 128, 130
Cotter; J.B.F., 87, 97
Covert; Col., 110
Covert; F.P., 93
Covert; H., 93
Coverts, 122
Craig; Robert, 146
Cramahe; T.H., 6
Crawford; Angus, 93
Croft; J., 128
Crofton; W.G., 111
Crosson; H., 128
Crosson; W., 127
Crouter; Abraham, 89, 99
Culver; Joel, 12
Cuthbert; James, 128, 145

D

Davis; J., 94
Danforth; Asa, 11, 12
Deane; Noah, 13
Derry; ——, 129
Dobson; P., 128
Doney; ——, 128
Draper; William H., 59
Drope; James, 145
Duignan; T., 129
Dubean; Jos., 145
Dumble; H., 94
Dumble; W., 128, 145
Duncan; A., 128
Duncan; H., 145
Dyer; ——, 96

E

Easton & Wright, 115
Eddy; Manchester, 45
Edgecombe; George, 87, 108, 127
Elliott; Rev. H., 145
Elliott; T., 127
Elmsey; ——, 15
Evans; Thomas, 119, 120
Ewing; Benjamin, 47
Eyre; Thomas, 115, 145, 146

F

Falkner; Henry, 93
Falkner; W., 63
Farmin; Jacob, 46
Ferris; David, 13
Field; John, 128, 145
Finlayson; C.S., 93
Firmin; Jacob, 43
Fisher; J., 95
Fleming; Sir Sanford, 111
Fleming; Thomas, 14
Fletcher; Alexander, 42
Fletcher; J., 145
Foley; Mr., 112
Fraser; Alexander, 7, 151
Frazer; Archibald, 59, 66, 128

G

Gamble & Boulton, 113
Gamble; Clark, 113
Garratt; W.A.,
Gee; John, 145
Gerome; Asahel, 13
Gerrans; ——, 127
Gifford; Humphrey, 13
Gifford; Samuel, 13
Gilchrist; Dr. John, 47, 58, 59
Gilchrist; Dr. James, 145
Gilchrist; J.A., 129, 145
Gillbard; Thomas, 54, 145
Gillbard; William, 128, 145
Goheen; Thomas, 13
Goldstone; Dr. George, 129
Goodeve & Corrigal, 115
Goodeve, G.M., 93, 120, 128, 130, 146
Gordon; James, 145
Graham & Minaker, 43
Grant; ——, 15
Graveley & Jackson, 115
Graveley; William, 92, 93, 128
Gray; ——, 128
Greeley; Aaron, 8, 9, 11, 12, 14, 15, 20, 24, 151

Greeley; Susan, 43
Green; Rev. Anson, 56, 57
Greenleaf; J.D., 127

Grieve; Messers, 127
Grieves; William, 145
Griffes; William,, 13
Griffins; William, 13
Grigg; William, 87, 95, 97
Grover; John, 47
Guillet; Edwin Clarence, 17, 63, 151
Guillet; John, 128, 145

H

Hagerman; Abraham, 13
Hagerman; Isaac, 13
Haldimand; General, 6
Hales; Edward, 95
Hales; H., 128
Hall; Isiah, 34, 129
Halliday; Andrew, 128, 145
Ham; George, 56, 60, 71, 82, 92, 94, 97, 99, 100, 110, 125
Ham; N.G., 110
Hambly; W., 8
Hamby; ——, 24
Hamilton; George, 108, 127
Hammond; W.W., 93
Hamilton; Henry, 6
Hancock; P.,145
Hancock; W.G., 127
Hare; Richard, 42
Hargraft; Mr., 100
Harison; Nathaniel, 13
Harriman; Dr., 28, 29
Harris; Boltus (Bolton), 13
Harris; Margaret, 30
Harris; Myndert, 8, 30
Harris; Peggy, 48
Harris; Joseph, 13
Harper; W.F., 93
Hart; George, 97
Hart; S.P., 87
Harvey; Thomas, 128, 145
Hathaway; William, 64
Hawkey; Anthony, 128, 145
Hawkins; J., 127
Hayden; Rev. William, 98
Hayden; Mrs., 98
Haynes; Edwin R., 148, 149
Haynes; Mrs., 148
Helms; J., 60
Helm; John, 127, 139
Henry; Robert, 50, 51, 56, 60, 63, 64, 68, 87, 97, 122, 125

Herchimer; Lawrence, 49
Herriman; Lawrence, 49
Herriman; Bethany, 27
Herriman; Bathnia, 22
Herriman; Dr., 24, 25, 26
Herriman; Diadama, 27
Herriman; Nathaniel, 13, 17, 19, 20, 21, 22, 44, 46
Hey; James, 115
Hicks; Joshua (Hix), 13
Hitchins; William, 108, 127
Hobart; M.T., 127
Hobart; M.F., 145
Hollowell; Thomas, M.D., 145
Holman; J., 128
Holywell; T., 129
Hooey; John, 127, 145
Hooey; Stuart, 145
Hope; Colonel, 6
Horton; N., 128, 145
Hossack; James, 128, 145
House; Franklin, 128, 145
Howard; —, 128
Huff; ——, 127
Hull; Eli C., 13, 129
Hunter; Peter, 34, 48
Hurst; J.F., 115, 128, 145
Hutchinson; J., 127

I

Iredel; Mr., 8
Irwin; Samuel, 127, 145

J

Jackson; H.H., 128
James; C.C., 23, 24
Jarvis; William, 34
Jeffrey; Andrew, 71, 82, 94, 115, 120, 145
Jessupp; Rev. H.B., 145
Jewell; Thomas, 145
Johnson; Sir John, 4
Jonathan; E., 93
Jones; Augustus, 4, 8, 12, 14, 15, 18, 23, 30, 151
Jones; Elias, 11, 13, 19, 20, 22, 30, 31, 42, 45, 48, 49, 52, 124
Jones; H.W., 93
Jones; Pevoy, 14
Jones; T.M., 59
Judge; Thomas, 128, 145

K

Keeler; Joseph A., 47
Keeler; Joseph, 7, 11, 12, 25, 43

Kells; W.H., 129
Kelly; John, 47
Kennedy; A.S., 145
Kennedy; John, 115, 128
Kernan; Father, 99
Kershaw; Thomas, 145
Ketchum; Rev. Mr., 66
Kewin; Patrick, 145
King Edward VII, 1
King George III, 61
King George IV, 140
King George V, 1
Kittridge; Dr. Timothy, 45, 46, 51, 56, 122
Kittson; W.H., 111, 112, 121
Knowles; William, 145

L

Ladu; Rev. S.W., 145
Lafontaine; Louis, 134
Lambert; James, 87, 88, 89, 95
Lambton; John George, 103
Lampman; Archibald, 26
Lapp; Frank, 25
Lapp; Jeremiah, 46, 51, 56
LaRocque; Francois Antoine, 56
Laurie; John, 93
Laurie; William, 145
Lawder; W., 99, 129
Lewis; Sylvester, 127, 145
Lockhead; John, 128, 145
Logan; F., 115
Lord Durham, 103
Lord Dorchester, 4, 6
Losee; Joseph J., 47
Lovekin; Richard, 42
Lower; J.A., 151
Lynn; J., 129

M

Madden; Rev. Thomas, 47
Mallory; Caleb, 47
Mann; J., 127
Marsh; Benjamin, 42, 93
Marshell; J.C., 127
Martin; Moses, 13, 18, 19, 20
Marvine; Samuel, 13
MacKechnie; Stuart E., 120, 125, 126
MacDonald; Alexander, 124, 125
MacDonald; Donald, 124
MacDonnell; Donald, 48, 49
Mackenzie; James, 52
Mackenzie; Kenneth, 68, 92, 97
MacKenzie; William Lyon, 93
Macbean & Strong, 115

McAllister; A., 127
McAllister; Daniel, 151
McBean; Arthur, 128, 146
McCallum; Peter, 60, 128, 146
McCarty; John, 60, 92, 94, 96, 120, 128
McConnell; J., 127
McCutcehon; James, 111
McDonald; Archibald, 58, 129, 146
McDonald; Lieut., 93
McDonald; Colonel, 48
McDonald; ——, 45
McDonald; Donald, 100, 101
McDonell; Alexander, 48, 51, 54, 56
McDonell; Mr., 56
McDowell; Rev. Robert, 13, 47
McGarvey; J., 93
McGill; Hon. Peter, 125
McGran; James, 129, 146
McIntosh; Capt. C., 64
McKechnie; S.E., 128
McKenning; Samuel S., 47
McKennedy; Michael, 146
McKenny; M., 128
McKeown; ——, 127
McKeyes; Barnabus, 47
McKeyes; Daniel, 13, 18, 19, 20
McKinley; ——, 128
McLenhan; J., 109, 127
McLeod; Rev. Donald, 128, 146
McManus; ——, 128
McMurtry; T., 129
Means; Richard, 146
Meredith; H.H., 93
Merriman; Joel, 42
Mewburn; James, Jr., 93
Miller; Rev. Matthew, 66
Milne; A., 128, 139
Milne; W., 127
Mitchell; John, 128, 146
Monjeau; John, 45, 51, 54, 122
Morgan; Charles H., 92, 101, 120
Morgan; Peter, 115, 120
Morrow; Matthew, 146
Morrow; Thomas, 146
Moscrept; Andrew, 146
Munro; S., 127
Munroe; R., 102
Munson; A.C., 127, 146
Murray; General, 5, 6
Murray; ——, 121
Myers; Captain, 25
Mungo; (Mongeau), 45

N

Nelles; Rev. S., 146
Newton; J., 127
Newton; P., 127
Newton; W., 127
Nickerson; Annie, 19
Nickerson; Catherine, 21
Nickerson; David, 21
Nickerson; Eluid, 14, 17, 18, 19, 20, 21, 25, 31, 43, 44, 45, 46, 51
Nickerson; Enos, 21
Nickerson; Ephriam, 21
Nickerson; Eunice, 21
Nickerson; John, 21, 46
Nickerson; Levi, 21
Nickerson; Roger N., 19
Nickerson; Mary, 21, 45
Nickerson; Nathaniel, 19, 21
Nickerson; Nicholas, 19
Nickerson; Thomas, 19
Nickerson; William, 19
Nicholson; Elias, 23, 24
Nicholson; Eluid, 24
Nichols; H.E., 93
Nihil; P., 127
Nixon; George A., 115, 127, 146
Nixon; J., 128
Noble; John, 128, 146
Norris; James, 47
Norton & Musser, 95
Nugen; John, 14, 48, 49, 124

O

Owston; C.J., 93

P

Patterson; David M., 111
Paton; A., 121, 128
Payne; William, 127, 146
Parker; Samuel, 14
Pearce; J., 128
Perino; Ranna, 14
Perring; Frederick, 14
Pearson; William, 128
Perry; Charles, 58, 93, 109
Perry; Ebenezer, 21, 46, 51, 56, 58, 59, 60, 63, 64, 68, 71, 82, 87, 88, 89, 90, 92, 94, 97, 119, 120, 122, 127, 128
Perry; George, 139, 145
Peters; John, 47
Pettits, ——, 29
Pierce; George, 93
Plews; ——, 127

P

Plunkett; J., 127
Pomeroy Brothers, 146
Pomeroy; Charles, 127, 146
Pomeroy; W., 127
Pool; (Poor), C., 128, 146
Powell; Ephriam, 54, 58
Powell; O., 127
Powell; Mrs. W.F., 146
Pratt; Thomas, 127, 146
Prince Albert, 101
Prince Philip, 148
Pringle; Alexander, 128, 146
Purdy; Gilbert, 14
Purdy; Joseph, Sr., 14
Purser; Matthew, 95, 108, 127

Q

Queen Elizabeth II, 148, 149
Queen Victoria, 92, 97, 101, 129, 147

R

Ralls; C.P., 24, 25
Radcliffe; Jas., 63
Ratcliff; Thomas, 108
Regan; Patrick, 146
Reid; H.S., 105
Reid; William, 21
Richardson; Benjamin, 42
Richardson; Samuel, 146
Roberts; John, 146
Robins; Rev. Paul, 146
Robinson; J., 127
Robinson; Hon. Peter, 56
Rogers; Captain, 94
Rogers; David McGregor, 15, 34, 35
Rogers; Idell, 17, 18, 25
Rogers; R.D., 93
Root; ——, 93
Ross; D., 128
Ross; John, 46
Rubidge; Alfred, 68, 94, 95, 108
Rubidge; Lieut., 109
Rubidge; F.P., 66, 68
Rundle; H., 128
Russell; Mr., 123, 124
Russell; George, 127
Russell; John, 128, 146
Russell; Hon. Peter, 30
Ruttan; Henry, 51, 57, 58, 66, 81, 99, 148
Ruttan; Henry J., 93
Ruttan; Richard, 129, 146
Ryerson; Rev. Egerton, 108

S

Saunders; Cpl., 93
Salisbury; Thomas, 97, 129, 146
Scott; Thomas, 139, 146
Scott; W.G., 127
Secor; A., 127, 146
Shaw; ——, 20
Simcoe; John Graves, 5, 6, 11, 12, 24, 37, 41, 47, 48, 134, 151
Simmons; ——, 127
Sinclair; R., 115
Sisson; Z., 95
Smades; Luke, 14
Smith; (Surveyor Gen.), 8
Smith; Elias, 15, 42
Smith; D.W., 11
Smith; John, 146
Smith; Sidney, 129, 146, 148
Smith; William, 146
Snell; Rev. I., 146
Snow; P., 146
Solomon; Richard, 95, 108
Solomon; William, 99
Soper; Leonard, 42
Sprague; Foster S., 94, 95
Spencer; George, 60
Spencer; Hazelton, 5
Spencer; John, 21, 46, 51, 56
Standcliffe; Stanborough P., 14, 18, 19, 20
Standley; ——, 128
Stanton; Eldridge, 47
Starling & Keeler, 95
Stephen; Abner, 14
Stephens; George, 127, 146
Stevens; Abner, 14
Stewart; Alexander, 146
Stickles; H., 127
Stiles; Lewis, 47, 124
Storms; Gilbert, 14
Strachan; (John), 70
Strong; W., 120, 128
Sutherland; Rev. D., 5
Sutherland; John, 128, 146
Swain; J., 128

T

Taylor; Rev. L., 146
Tennery; J., 129
Terry; Henry, 115, 120, 128, 146
Thompson; G., 128, 146
Thompson; J.W., 129, 146
Throop; Benjamin, 54, 58, 59, 63, 64, 68, 92, 108

Throop; Robert H., 93, 129, 139, 145, 146
Tigh; J., 127
Timlin; Rev. Michael, 146
Tobin; W., 127
Tremain; J.E., 108, 115
Tremain; W., 54, 93, 115, 119, 120
Trimble; James, 87, 94, 96, 97
Trudeau; Francois, 54, 56
Tubbs; Daniel, 14
Tubbs; Frederick, 14
Tubbs; Isiah, 25
Tuttle; Stephen, 14, 18, 19
Tuttle; Elizabeth, 19, 20

U

Usher family, 21

V

Vandusen; Rev. C., 146
Van Ingen; W., 120, 128
Vannatto; John, 14
Vaughan; John, 14, 34
Vaughan; Nancy, 12
Vernat; John, 14
Vosper; George, 146

W

Waldie; ——, 45
Waite; Samantha, 29
Wallis; John, 12
Wallace, 114, 120
Wallace; Patrick, 125, 127, 128, 130, 132
Warren, Capt. Edward, 93, 94
Ward; Thomas, 47, 62, 63, 105
Weller; Asa, 42
Weller; William, 60, 82, 94, 96, 99, 102, 105, 114, 116, 117, 121, 139, 145, 146, 148
Wells; Mrs. Margaret, 43, 45, 51
Whitaker; J., 95
White; Josiah, 45, 127
White; Liberty, 14
Whittier; ——, 22, 25
Williams; James, 46, 51, 56, 122
Williams; Nathan, 14, 21, 22, 46
Wilson; J.L., 129
Wilson; James, 121, 146
Wolcott; Roger, 12, 14
Wolf; ——, 5

Y

Young; James, 60, 127

End of Index